Cambridge Elements

Elements in Evolutionary Economics

MAKING SENSE OF ECONOMIC CHANGE

Intentionality, Action Plans, and Evolution

Félix-Fernando Muñoz
Autonomous University of Madrid

CAMBRIDGE
UNIVERSITY PRESS

CAMBRIDGE
UNIVERSITY PRESS

Shaftesbury Road, Cambridge CB2 8EA, United Kingdom

One Liberty Plaza, 20th Floor, New York, NY 10006, USA

477 Williamstown Road, Port Melbourne, VIC 3207, Australia

314–321, 3rd Floor, Plot 3, Splendor Forum, Jasola District Centre,
New Delhi – 110025, India

Cambridge University Press is part of Cambridge University Press & Assessment,
a department of the University of Cambridge.

We share the University's mission to contribute to society through the pursuit of
education, learning and research at the highest international levels of excellence.

www.cambridge.org
Information on this title: www.cambridge.org/9781009558082

DOI: 10.1017/9781009558105

When citing this work, please include a reference to the DOI 10.1017/9781009558105

First published 2026

A catalogue record for this publication is available from the British Library

*A Cataloging-in-Publication data record for this Element is available
from the Library of Congress*

ISBN 978-1-009-55808-2 Hardback
ISBN 978-1-009-55809-9 Paperback
ISSN 2514-3573 (online)
ISSN 2514-3581 (print)

Making Sense of Economic Change

Intentionality, Action Plans, and Evolution

Elements in Evolutionary Economics

DOI: 10.1017/9781009558105
First published online: June 2026

Félix-Fernando Muñoz
Autonomous University of Madrid

Author for correspondence: Félix-Fernando Muñoz, felix.munoz@uam.es

Abstract: Intentionality is a key constituent of human action in a world of pervasive uncertainty and provisional knowledge. Intentionality provides meaning to the action plans of the agents that interact within a socioeconomic system. Social interaction produces orders that, although more than the sum of individual actions, acquire direction imprinted by the intentional content and structure of the courses of action of the individuals and organizations that interact within the system. Although many of the consequences of interaction may be unintended and even opposite to agents' intentions, the evolution of the system is not entirely blind. Explaining why and how this can be so is the purpose of this Element.

Keywords: intentionality, action plans, complex evolving systems, novelties, emergence

JEL classifications: A12, B40, B52, O10

ISBNs: 9781009558082 (HB), 9781009558099 (PB), 9781009558105 (OC)
ISSNs: 2514-3573 (online), 2514-3581 (print)

Contents

Human action is purposeful behavior.

(Mises, Human Action)

In the beginning there was a plan.

(Loasby, Knowledge, Institutions and Evolution in Economics)

1 Introduction

1.1 The Context

We live in a complex world in which uncertainty is pervasive. Our knowledge about the connections between physical–natural and social phenomena is limited, and our ignorance of the future, beyond the inertia of the systems, which makes the immediate future look very similar to the present moment, is almost total.[1] And yet, in these circumstances, we humans are impelled to act, to make decisions about courses of action that will produce effects in the imagined future under the hypothesis that if we follow those courses of action, we will achieve (produce) states of the world more desirable for us. The valuation of those states of affairs triggers our interaction with the physical–natural and social systems. Action is intentional; it pursues specific goals (ends), which give meaning to action and make it intelligible, "rational."

The outcome of social interaction implies the emergence of spontaneous properties and orders that transform the nature of physical and social reality. To the extent that these emergent properties are beyond the intention of individuals and organizations, the socioeconomic process appears to be a blind process. However, and this is our main claim in this Element, it is not, since the whole process is based on the interactive deployment of a multitude of intentional courses of action. Social interaction, which is at the basis of the structural transformation of social systems, ends up producing orders that, although they are more than the aggregate of individual actions, acquire a direction that is imprinted on them by the intentional content and structure of the courses of action of the individuals and organizations that interact within the system. Explaining why and how this can be so is the purpose of this Element.

Intentionality is a prominent feature of conscious human action.[2] According to Searle (1983, p. 1), "intentionality is that property of many mental states and

[1] All human knowledge is conjectural in character. Our knowledge of the future is as conjectural as our knowledge of the past. Ignorance is not total because of the role, for example, of institutions (including science), which operate as scaffolds for establishing new conjectures. Moreover, institutions circumscribe the range of possible future actions, thereby reducing complete ignorance about the future, at least in the short run.

[2] For the distinction between conscious and unconscious action, see Mises (1949, Chap. 1). Intentionality is not the same as conscious, because many conscious states (e.g., anxiety about snakes) are not intentional.

events by which they are directed at or about or of objects and states of affairs in the world."[3] Intentionality makes it possible for our thoughts, beliefs, desires, hopes, and fears to refer to things outside ourselves, whether present or, more typically, in the future. *Intentionality is directness*; there is no meaningful action without intention. Examples of intentional actions include raising one's arm to vote, signing a contract, making a promise, buying stocks, and producing iron, among others.

People have partial and local (and usually erroneous) knowledge of their present circumstances. When we refer to the future, things are even worse. Any act presupposes a projection into the future. Thus, economic agents must imagine future states of the world that they deem possible and consider how to introduce changes to improve their actual personal condition (e.g., an increase in well-being); consequently, they act purposively. Purposive action is driven by goals and expectations and is informed by past experiences. In other words, economic agents (individuals and organizations) do not act in a vacuum or purely based on random processes; instead, their actions are driven by intentions that shape the direction and nature of economic change. The interactive deployment of purposive action leads to innovations (novelties), adaptation, and structural change. However, as noted before, while intentions shape microlevel actions, the aggregate outcomes are often emergent orders and may deviate from individual expectations. This duality – where intentionality drives change and leads to unintended macro-level phenomena – captures the essence of the relationship between evolutionary complex systems and intentionality. At the micro level, it is straightforward to understand the ends or goals of action and how means and actions are ordered (discovered, even invented) to achieve them. The role of intentionality becomes less clear when considering the meso and macro levels of analysis. In those other levels, emergence and complexity manifest, blurring the role of intentionality at the social level. This is why some authors consider evolution a blind (Darwinian-like) process (Hodgson & Knudsen, 2006). However, if social processes are blind, how can individuals attach meaning to them? Although we will address this question at the end of this Element, we can anticipate (provisionally) the answer: for us, intentionality provides individuals and organizations with meaning to navigate and adapt to an evolving, complex economic environment.[4]

[3] Intentional states and events are not just mental acts.

[4] In their work on technological change and firm behavior, Dosi and Nelson (1994) describe how firms intentionally engage in search and innovation processes.

1.2 Intentionality, a Missing Driver in the Explanation of Economic Change

In a world of uncertainty in which action is needed, rational human action must be based on reasons to act (Searle, 2001). (As we will see, reasons for action bind together concepts such as goals, purposeful action, intentionality, rationality, and efficiency.) The idea of intentionality dates to Scholastic philosophy. However, Brentano (1874) incorporated the concept of intentionality into modern philosophy. For him, the "intentional relationship" describes a subjective behavior toward something that may not be real but is present as an object.[5] In simpler terms, *intentionality is the mind's aboutness* – its capacity to be *directed toward* something. Mental acts – like believing, hoping, fearing, desiring, judging – are always about something. They have content or are directed toward objects, even if those objects do not exist, like unicorns or fictional characters. In Brentano's view, mental phenomena contain their object within themselves, not in a spatial sense, but in an "immanent" way. On the contrary, physical phenomena do not exhibit intentionality – for Brentano, this fundamentally separates the mental from the physical. Moreover, finally, all and only mental phenomena have intentionality.

Anscombe (1957) is a primary reference for the concept of intentionality. Although she does not provide a singular, formal definition of intentionality, she investigates the concept through the lens of intentional action, emphasizing the importance of context and the agent's perspective. A central tenet of Anscombe's analysis is that an action is intentional if the question "Why?," asked in a particular sense, applies to it. If an agent can provide a reason or purpose for their action, the action qualifies as intentional.[6] Anscombe also distinguishes between practical and theoretical knowledge through the concept of *direction of fit* (see Sections 2 and 3). In theoretical knowledge, our beliefs aim to match the world (mind-to-world direction of fit). In practical knowledge, our intentions aim to shape the world to match our desires (world-to-mind direction of fit). She illustrates this with the example of a shopping list: If the

[5] In a famous passage, Brentano says that "every mental phenomenon is characterized by what the Scholastics called the intentional (or mental) inexistence of an object . . . Each one includes something as an object within itself, although not always in the same way." Brentano (1874 [1995], p. 68)

[6] Anscombe introduces the concept that actions are intentional under certain descriptions but not others. In the previous example, while the action is intentional under the description "pumping water," it may not be intentional under descriptions like "contracting muscles" or "making a rhythmic motion." This highlights the significance of the agent's perspective and the context in which the action occurs.

list represents what one intends to buy, failing to purchase an item is not a false belief but a failure in execution.

Brentano's concept of intentionality and Anscombe's work have significantly influenced contemporary discussions on the philosophy of action and the contemporary philosophy of mind. The concept of intentionality is central to discussions about mental representation, consciousness, and the nature of mental states. Philosophers like John Searle have explored intentionality in the context of language and consciousness, while others have examined its implications for artificial intelligence and cognitive science.[7] Among the various interpretations, those that best align with our understanding of intentionality are the ones proposed by Bratman (1999, 2007) and Searle (1983). A precedent for what will be discussed here, as established by Miller et al. (1960), provides a clear connection between plans and the structure of human behavior. We will link intentionality with the economic action structure through the concept of the action plan.

Given their heroic assumptions and methodological limitations, mainstream economics is not the most suitable approach for addressing intentionality, action, and emergent properties.[8] We need a different approach or try to integrate different but compatible approaches to insert intentionality into our research on the evolution and structural change of complex systems. The integrative approach we use for this purpose in this Element is what we have referred to elsewhere as the *action plan approach* (Encinar & Muñoz, 2006; Muñoz & Encinar, 2014a). A way to connect intentionality and economics is via planned action. Intentionality is embodied in agents' goals of action, content, and the goals' sequential and hierarchical structure. Agents link projectively actions and means to those goals or ends; thus, our study on the role of intentionality is an investigation into planned action. In Section 3, we introduce the action plan approach, based on Rubio de Urquía's writings. As we will demonstrate, this approach offers a coherent analytical framework for addressing the emergence and evolution of socioeconomic systems. The action plan approach integrates intentional categories of human action – beliefs, goals, strategies, actions, and plans – into a network of systems and subsystems. In this way, at the micro level, a plan of action forms a system of actions and goals that guide and provide meaning to agents' actions. At the meso level, it interacts with other subsystems, which include others' action plans. And at the macro level, we can understand the economy as an ecology of plans (Wagner, 2012).

[7] Intentionality can be understood in many other ways (see Paredes Martín (2007)), but due to space constraints, we will not enter into philosophical disputes. In all cases, they refer to *directness*.

[8] Due to space constraints, we cannot discuss this issue here. Wagner (2010) provides a good summary.

The action plan approach is not a new concept. The concept of an action plan has been present in economics since at least the Marginalist Revolution, as a line of thought that deals directly, or ultimately, with action, and not only with the relationships between mere objects (Arthur, 2023). Indeed, for authors such as Menger (1871), Mises (1949), Schutz (1951), Lachmann (1951), and Boulding (1981), as well as the Austrian tradition,[9] Economics is a theory of human action in a social context. This societal dimension of human action will allow us, as we will see, to reconstruct, based on the Austrian tradition combined with Evolutionary and Complexity economics, the intentional character of economic activity. The point of departure is the fact that "human action is purposeful action" (Mises, 1949, p. 11).[10] It is this tradition that animates this Element.

In most economic theories, particularly in the mainstream, intentionality and planned action are missing drivers in explaining actual economic activity. Goals and courses of action are given and ideally identified and connected with known outcomes. Agents can perfectly anticipate the consequences of their choices in terms of gains or losses in well-being (including profits). When this is not the case, such as in situations of choice under uncertainty, these situations are not really so, as Shackle (1979) explains. Models such as those of Savage (1951) and Kahneman and Tversky (1979) only add technicalities to consider "uncertainty." However, they are closed models (Loasby, 2003) in the sense that to operate (e.g., maximize), they need to have perfectly delimited the decision sets and the probability allocation system. However, how do the real novelties (scientific–technical, but also market) fit in there? This problem deeply interested Schumpeter, but he could not give a clear solution, which irremediably left it beyond economic explanation, giving rise to what Encinar and Muñoz (2006) have called Schumpeter's Paradox.

Why is intentionality so important? Because intentionality is a key constituent element of planning. Intentionality gives directness, coherence, stability, and, above all, sense to action. Planned action is guided action. Only on this basis, at the micro level, can one speak of the rationality and efficiency of the planned action. Of course, there is room for other types of unplanned action that, in unique contexts, can be very relevant. Thus, reflex and unconscious actions

[9] This is the case of the causal-genetic method in Austrian economics, pioneered by Carl Menger. It is a way to understand complex economic phenomena by logically decomposing them into their simplest elements (individual actions, desires, beliefs) and tracing how more complex market outcomes evolve or emerge from these purposeful, intentional beginnings, focusing on the *why* and *how* rather than just *what*. The method emphasizes understanding the temporal generation of economic events, driven by human action, subjectivism, and the creative roles of entrepreneurs, in contrast to purely mathematical equilibrium models (see Vanberg, 2022).

[10] Contrary to the neoclassical conception in which agent behavior is "rational, maximizing," increased realism implies "purposive, adaptive, biased, myopic" agents. See Table I in Axtell and Farmer (2025, p. 203).

can save our lives (such as a defensive action or a timely escape) or lead to disastrous results (like panic). Of course, emotions play a vital role in our daily behavior. However, according to purposes or goals, a rational action can be the object of rational analysis. Economics employs two central categories: means and objectives. Moreover, it is the objectives that agents pursue in their daily activities. Moreover, these objectives do not have to be given in the sense of Robbins (1932), nor do they have to be alien to the interest of economists. An openness to the objectives allows us to examine the relationship between the dynamics (individual and social) of the objectives and the actions deployed, which generate emergent properties in evolving systems due to interaction.

1.3 Structure of the Element

Section 2 addresses the pervasive presence and consequences of uncertainty in human affairs, the projective character of human action, and the analytical role of intentionality. Section 3 introduces the pivotal concept of an action plan. This concept integrates intentionality as a constitutive element of planned action, the one that gives meaning to human action. Other concepts typically from evolutionary economics, such as rules, capabilities, and routines, are connected to action plans. The section concludes by examining the relationship between intentionality, rationality, and efficiency. Complex evolving systems result from human and societal interaction; thus, Section 4 introduces interaction and the drivers of economic change, such as entrepreneurship. In this context, we address the role of institutions and the concept of evolutionary efficiency. Section 5 connects all previous elements to form an analytical framework that explains the economy as an evolutionary process. This process results from interactions at different levels of analysis (micro–meso–macro) within an ecology of plans. We finish with some final remarks and a proposal for further research.

2 Intentionality

2.1 A World of Uncertainty, Complexity, and Ignorance

Human action is projective. Agents (individuals and organizations, such as firms) judge their situation at a moment in time, in the light of their experience and previous expectations, and imagine, in a subjective sense, better possible states in the immediate and distant future. They also imagine courses (sequences) of actions that use scarce resources to reach those better situations. In this sense, agents allocate resources according to their preferences, ensuring the best use of available resources. Of course, better future states depend not only on their own decisions and actions but also on those of other agents with whom they interact in a social environment. One crucial problem arises at this point: Human beings do not know the future course of events. Humans' knowledge is partial, local, and provisional; moreover, their ability to collect and process information is also limited, and it cannot be ruled out – instead, it is the "default state" – that agents suffer from all kinds of cognitive biases, as behavioral economics shows (Earl, 2022; Gigerenzer, 2008; Thaler, 2015). In any case, the universe is so complex, with so many connections and a continuous flow of novelties, that radical uncertainty is pervasive (Loasby, 1999).

In such a context of uncertainty and partial ignorance, the fundamental economic problem is a problem of knowledge.[11] However, the foundations of knowledge are always problematic, as Loasby (2000) has shown. Inductive thinking is an obvious way to proceed in this type of situation. Induction is always incomplete, and there is no way to demonstrate the truth of any general empirical proposition about reality (Popper, 1959). Consequently, human knowledge and behavior patterns are always conjectural, and conjectures go far beyond what we know. Moreover, when a pattern of behavior fails (but, as we will see, error plays a key role in evolutionary processes), it is almost impossible to demonstrate which conjecture fails. Some additional facts compound the problem: (1) humans have limited mental capacity (Simon, 1955), a limitation that compels agents to adopt simplified representations and simplified procedures that cannot be optimally chosen and often rely on linkages that cannot be classed as logical; (2) the continuous emergence of innovations (both exogenous and endogenous) adds obstacles to complete knowledge (Schumpeter, 1947); and (3) agents usually pursue conflicting purposes, that range from rivalry between similar plans of action to contradictory notions about appropriate ways of arranging human affairs (Earl, 2022; Simon, 1983). Thus, the background and point of departure for economics should be the problem of knowledge in a context of pervasive uncertainty, a state of affairs in which agents cannot assign probabilities to events that seem likely or plausible to them within their planning horizon. The complexity of socioeconomic systems, the interdependencies with their natural elements, and human choices, put this task far beyond human rationality. However, human beings have "both a psychological and practical need *to understand*, and where possible *to predict*, the behaviour of these systems" (Loasby, 1989: vi, italics added). Paradoxically, uncertainty creates opportunities for economic development: It is the precondition of intelligence. Rational choice theory excludes

[11] According to Witt (2003) economics is not (solely) concerned about economizing scarce; rather it is accumulative problem solving and knowledge generation on the one side, a successive creation of new problems on the other.

intelligence and entrepreneurship; we only need automata. In contrast, in actual situations, "people must create their structures for interpretation and decision or find some ready-made structure that they are prepared to adapt" (Loasby, 2007, p. 33).

Knight states that agents form categories based on significant similarities, ignoring differences they believe to be irrelevant and conditional on "the purpose or problem in view" (Knight, 1921, p. 206). Knight also claims that "the existence of a problem of knowledge depends on the future being different from the past, while the possibility of the solution of the problem depends on the future being like the past" (Knight, 1921, p. 313). Therefore, all decisions involve a selective mapping from past to future, where the selection principles are conjectural. In contrast to rational choice models, agents often lack the time and computational capabilities to make an optimal decision in every situation. Rationality must be applied very selectively. Within conventional economics, bounded rationality is often viewed as a form of cognitive failure. However, that interpretation diverts attention from the truly remarkable human capability to create and use patterns. This pattern-making capability appears to be more helpful than a high level of logical skills (Gigerenzer, 2021). Moreover, the rational choices that economists – mainly mainstream economists – attribute to economic agents exhibit no signs of purposeful reasoning. They are mechanisms programmed to provide optimal responses to changes in the circumstances (constraints) in which those agents are placed. On the contrary, the limitations imposed by uncertainty compel agents to create or adopt representations and simplified procedures that cannot be optimally chosen and often rely on linkages that cannot be classed as logical.

2.2 People as Scientists

Even though we cannot know what and how the future course of the most immediate events in our lives will look like, we are compelled to act to reach our desired goals. However, to the extent that no purposeful action is possible without "knowledge of the future," how do we proceed in such a context? The American psychologist George A. Kelly proposed a helpful metaphor for describing and analyzing human behavior: Men deal with the future as scientists do with their research on physical phenomena.[12] Kelly's proposal departs from a realist ontology in which the universe is real and not "a figment of our imaginations" (Kelly, 1963, p. 7). Next, Kelly establishes three main

[12] Kelly's theory resembles Adam Smith's psychological theory of scientific progress (Smith, 1795 [1980]) and Popper's (1959) methodology of science. More recently, under "the growth-of-knowledge" tradition that has adopted Kelly's lead, we can include economists such as Loasby (1971, 2009), Earl (1983, 1992), Harper (1996), and Earl and Muñoz (2027a).

hypotheses: (1) man is gradually coming to understand the universe; (2) the universe is nondecomposable (it is integral) but we treat it "as if" it is quasi-decomposable (see Simon, 1969) – men live only within a limited section of the universe and that span of time we recognize as our present; and (3) the universe is continually changing with respect to itself. And because life is an interaction, not a mere reaction, this implies increasing complexity.

According to Kelly, to deal with reality, men look at their world through personal (subjective) lenses, which he refers to as *constructs*. Constructs are patterns or templates that people create and impose to fit over the realities of the world. Kelly's central hypothesis is that all men behave *as scientists* whose motivation is, as well as the scientist's ultimate aim, "to predict and control" (Kelly, 1963, p. 5).[13] Men look at the world through their constructs using them as guides for action and then attempt to fit over the realities of which the world is composed. As in science, the fit is not always perfect, but "[e]ven a poor fit is more helpful than nothing at all" (Kelly, 1963, pp. 8–9), and without patterns, man cannot have a sense of it. Finally, constructs are tested regarding their predictive efficiency and are open to change or revision.

Of course, the personal viewpoints of different men are usually different, and other scientists' theoretical points of view are also different. As we will see in Section 4.3, this tendency to variety is a key property for the emergence of novelties and the growth of knowledge. Personal constructs correspond to scientific conjectures (e.g., theories) and, as in the Popperian system, any construct is transient. As scientists in their labs, men seek to improve their constructs by expanding their repertoire, modifying them to provide better fits, and subsuming them within superordinate constructs or systems. According to Kelly, constructs can be communicated and shared, at least to some extent, as scientific theories (see Ziman, 2000). This is so, even though they are tacit, usually implicit, and we are not always aware of the lenses through which we observe phenomena.

Another key feature of personal constructs is that it is possible to develop a detailed system of constructs without worrying about the inconsistencies in the system that specific peripheral facts would reveal. Given the quasi-decomposable nature of systems, inconsistencies can be handled using hierarchical thinking: People limit the realm and, for the time being, intransigent facts just outside the realm's borders. Humans must content themselves with a series of "miniature systems," each with its own realm or limited range of convenience. The same events can often be viewed in the light of two or more

[13] Contrary to Kelly, for Popper, the aim of science is to explain: to provide true explanations of reality.

systems, yet they do not belong to any specific system. Moreover, people's practical systems have foci and limited ranges of convenience, which would explain the retention of those systems even though they were not the most efficient ones.

A natural question here is, where do conjectures come from? We meet again to address the problems of induction, validation, and so on. For Kelly, changes in theories depend on *the stimuli's needs and motives*, but also depend, as Popper (1972) reminds us, on experiences that disappoint expectations. Here is the connection to intentionality. As in Smith's psychological theory of the emergence of science (see Sen, 2010), where the main reason that triggers curiosity is the human desire for mental tranquility, for Kelly, needs and motives operate as "internal irritants" (Kelly, 1963, pp. 36–37), and the strongest motive is to predict and control. We will see below that agents' action plans are, in reality, conjectures, guides for action elaborated by agents, and that the laboratory is reality, mediated by the market and other forms of interaction. But is not the economy in general and markets in particular experimental by their very nature?

2.3 Connections and the Mind

At an abstract level, it is connections between elements that make up a system (Loasby, 2001; Potts, 2000). The components of a system can be very diverse: physical objects that are arranged in unique ways (e.g., a hammer, which combines a shaft or handle with a mass, to strike more effectively); ideas and concepts, as in scientific theories and paradigms (Kuhn and Lakatos); conjectures (Popper); and, as will be the case in our analytical framework, actions and goals. Connections can be contemporaneous or unfold "dynamically" in a temporal sequence. Likewise, connected objects can be present at a moment in time (e.g., here and now, as this hammer), imagined in the future (e.g., the production plan for hammers), or linked in an abstract way (e.g., the concept of a hammer). This would be the case for courses of action related to the acting agent's expectations of a better (more desirable) future state. The system changes (evolves) when connections and elements change.

Many of the previous ideas have their correlation at the biological level. Like scientific hypotheses, agents' conjectures about future events arise from the new combination or recombination of connections between existing elements in a system. At a biological level, recombination can involve chemical molecules, DNA, and so on, but also, and this is the case that interests us the most, the neural connections of people's cones and brain areas (Fuster, 2003). Hayek (1952) was a pioneer in this issue. The human brain is a system of connections in which the elements are neurons and their networks; the system is determined by the connections, via dendrites and axons, between those neurons. At the beginning of the twentieth century, Ramón y Cajal first described this type of brain functioning and its key property: plasticity. Numerous explanations can be found in modern texts of physiology and neuroscience (Fuster, 2008). This architecture of the brain is reflected in how it classifies and orders information and converts it into knowledge, something Hayek already anticipated (Fuster, 2011). In economics, various authors, such as Loasby, have explained it.[14]

According to Fuster (2008), executive functions control action in the brain, more specifically in the prefrontal cortex. The executive function set is the preparation for actions. The set is attention-focused on the action to come. Attention is projected into the future and focuses on preparing executive networks for the execution of that action (2008, p. 347). From the set or motor attention derives the *intention to act*. Though intention may appear to precede the attention (in a teleological way), the conscious intention to perform an act, whether at the start of a sequence of actions or in the middle of it, may in fact precede the preparation set of the motor apparatus (2008, p. 348). Prefrontal networks can integrate percepts and actions of a high order of complexity (p. 268). The set includes not only the preparation of individual acts but also of sequences of them; that is, the preparation of a complete plan of sequential actions toward a goal (2008, p. 353). Accordingly, the plan, like the set, has a future perspective. Again, as we ponder the evident importance of the prefrontal cortex in planning, we encounter apparent teleology in the cortex. Indeed, its involvement in formulating and implementing plans of action seems dictated by future objectives and events. However, this apparent inversion of causality in the temporal domain can be explained by the preexistence in the frontal cortex of executive cognits or representations of plans that are somehow associated, at least fragmentarily, with the plan to be formulated and executed at a given time.[15] Empirical evidence in both animals and humans indicates that cognitive and emotional functions are distributed across the prefrontal cortex. Thus, the successful execution of a plan requires a prior

[14] The complex relationship between the brain and the mind has given rise to a vast amount of literature. In our case, in addition to the proto-theories of Adam Smith (1795) and Alfred Marshall (1868), we have the aforementioned works of Hayek, Popper (see Popper & Eccles, 1977), and Damasio (1994).

[15] According to Fuster (2008, p. 354), "we must assume that the plan is represented in the form of an executive frontal network ... that incorporates the schema of the plan, its essential action components, and its goal. We can further assume that the network representing the plan, as well as its components, is organized in hierarchical fashion." The failure to formulate plans, specifically new plans, is generally accepted as being a common feature of prefrontal syndromes.

conceptual scheme for the plan, preparation for each step in its implementation, and anticipation of its consequences.[16]

Knowledge is variable and subject to change due to the plasticity of the central nervous system. Plasticity and new combinations are key properties of the neural networks in the brain that enable learning. The connections between perception, attention, planning, and motor action are straightforward at the physiological level in humans. In economics, there is an interesting parallel between this way of understanding the human mind and the cognitive foundation of the economic agent (see Viale, 2027). This is evident in the tradition from Adam Smith to Jason Potts, passing through Marshall, Hayek, and Shackle, among many others. For example, connectivist principles are illustrated by the idea of connecting principles in Smith's (1795) *History of Astronomy*. In that work, Smith seeks to understand how people accept certain empirical propositions as true and develops a psychological theory of the emotional and aesthetic motivations and imaginative processes by which phenomena are gathered into categories and causally linked to other categories by the corresponding connecting principles. Smith analyses the psychological effects of "Wonder, Surprise, and Admiration" that trigger the way agents/people resolve their knowledge problems. The role Smith (1776[1976], p. 21) assigns to "philosophers and men of speculation" is precisely to envisage "new combinations." The effects of a knowledge-generating division of labor within the economy subsequently became his fundamental explanation of the wealth of nations. Error also plays a central role in Smith's account. The unexpected and the surprise may be perceived as a failure of the patterns imposed or of the connecting principles used. This apparent failure highlights the challenge of selecting suitable contexts of similarity as the basis for *intelligent action*.

A natural extension to economic modeling, which takes this connectivist approach seriously and generates a kind of homomorphism with the brain and other systems, can be found in Earl and Potts (2004). These authors go so far as to propose a connectivist reconstruction of the economic agent and the economy.[17] From this perspective of connections, the entire economic system can be recomposed from the point of view of connections (see, e.g., Beinhocker, 2006; Dopfer & Potts, 2009).

---

[16] A third major prefrontal function is executive attention, indispensable to planning and decision-making. Executive attention has three critical components, all three participants in the goal-directed temporal organization of action: (1) working memory, (2) preparatory set, and (3) inhibitory interference control (Fuster, 2008, p. 4).

[17] Following Earl (2003), the economic agent is completely reconstructed when all of his internal and external operational connections have been made completely explicit. Note that in a Walrasian general equilibrium model there is no room for true learning.

2.4 The Space of Representations

Agents try to make sense of the world by imposing patterns on it and then sticking to them if they are tolerably successful in allowing them to feel that they understand what they observe and experience (the basis for an efficiency criterion). Those patterns are the outcome of what Loasby (2007, p. 31) has called *connecting principles*. Connecting principles bind together perceptions, concepts, ideas, conjectures, and so on, and impose a logical structure that allows actual agents to apprehend reality, which, regardless of their fallible character, constitutes a guide for action. Thanks to imagination, it is possible to establish these connecting principles. Shackle (1972) stresses the role of imagination. Imagination – the ability to create, at a cognitive level, images or scenes that are not present in the perceptual field of the individual who articulates them – not only conceives new possibilities and choices that make a difference and demarcate subsystems and domains but also allows one to tame disorder across domains. A sense of "order and consistency" is a psychological necessity: patterns, as well as innovative ideas, must be imagined and "deemed possible" (Shackle, 1979, p. 26).

Thus, agents proceed by creating *selective connections* and building knowledge by making patterns of connections within systems to impose order and envisage new combinations in an evolutionary process, driven by human purpose, of competing and complementary conjectures. Conjectures and even theories can only fully explain systems that are less complex than themselves. They form networks of concepts and representations intended to match actual structures and are themselves confined to the *space of representations* of the agents. Nevertheless, their relationship to the real-world phenomena they are intended to interpret is inescapably uncertain. No human being can avoid this fact. In practice, both natural selection and the mind's selection among human ideas, artifacts, organizations, and institutions are based on characteristics that are successful within particular environments. And because all representations are incomplete, the opportunity cost of success is likely to include the absence of characteristics that would be essential for success in some other possible environments. On the other hand, every successful system has its characteristic way of failing, and even systems that survive may exhibit persistent pathologies, which may be fatal to some members of the relevant population. The population of entrepreneurs is a notable example; entrepreneurial failure is a natural conclusion from this conception of the mind in which the great majority of new combinations that can be imagined will turn out to be poor representations when deployed in external reality.

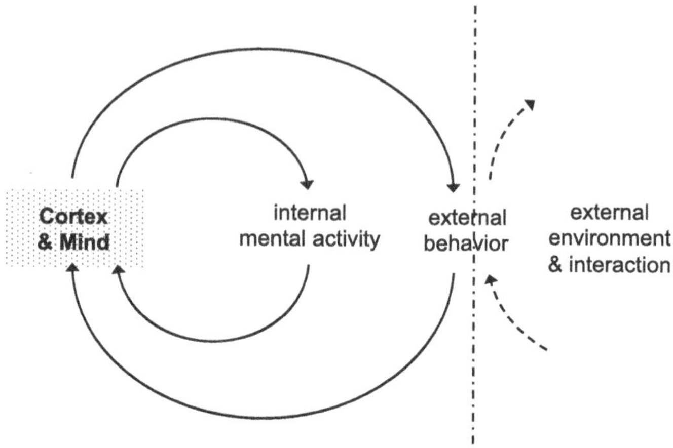

Figure 1 Internal mental activity and external behavior.
Based on Dopfer (2005, p. 24).

Representations take place in what some have called the *space of representations*, in the mind of each agent. Although the space of representations can have a physiological substrate in the brain, the connections and levels of interaction are so complex that the typical functions of the mind (representing, evaluating, and perceiving) are not located in a single brain area, although, as said above in Section 2.3, executive functions concentrate in the prefrontal cortex. This internal activity of the mind and brain is represented in Figure 1. Within it, the patterns of connections that will be tested in reality are formed, reinforcing the connections and/or recombinations that are perceived as successful when tested in external reality. In this space of references, internal to the subject, cognitive, ethical, and sociocultural dynamics converge.

The role of uncertainty is paradoxical. As Shackle emphazised, external change creates uncertainty; but is uncertainty what makes internally generated change possible? Problems – perceived inadequacies of existing patterns of interpretation, action deployed, and the final outcome – are also opportunities for imagining new patterns of interpretation and action that may be better fitted to the new circumstances. Loasby (1976, chap. 6) proposed the concept of "reference standards" as a key mechanism for coping with uncertainty. Reference standards allow "people to be motivated to search for comparators, to review plans, and to devise or import procedures that might generate novelty" (Loasby, 2007, p. 43).

As noted earlier, there is a role for error. The coexistence of systematic advantage and systematic deficiency is a common finding in experimental economics and psychology. If such results seem surprising, it is because inappropriate theories interpret them, and because economists have forgotten that opportunity costs (revealed by systematic deficiencies) are inherent in their professional activities. It is a notable merit of Gigerenzer and Selten (2001) investigation of "the adaptive toolbox" that they explicitly link the systematic advantages of "fast and frugal heuristics" within a particular domain to systematic errors outside that domain, even though the boundaries of the domain are often difficult to recognize by those using a specific heuristic.

2.5 The Role of Intentionality

Intention gives rise to intentional action. Perception and intentional action, or the intention to do something, are the two primary forms of intentionality, since they are the most elementary capacities of the mind to relate the organism to the world. For example, when we look at or listen to somebody or something, we do so with a specific intention. Also, when we turn our attention to the contexts and outcomes of action, we perceive the problems that give rise to the reworking of conjectures and the formulation of new plans of action.

According to Bratman, "intention is inextricably tied to the phenomena of plans and planning" (Bratman, 2007, p. 2). Purposeful action is characterized by *directness*. Intentionality is a very general notion that has to do with the *directedness of the mind*. Beliefs, hopes, fears, desires, and emotions are intentional states. Intentional states represent objects and states of affairs. Of course, not all mental states and events are intentional (e.g., forms of nervousness, bliss, or anxiety), but only those that are directed at something or are about something. Nor are all intentional states conscious (e.g., beliefs that have never been consciously formulated or considered).[18] In any case, although intentional states form the basis for intentionality, intentional states are not acts (not even acts of the mind). Any intentional action must fulfill the conditions of satisfaction. The specification of the content of an action is already a specification of the condition of satisfaction of that action. Regarding these conditions, Searle distinguishes between the representative (intentional) content and the *psychological mode*, depending on the kind of intentional state – belief, desire, or hope. Depending on the intentional mode, the direction of fit of intentional states differs. From the agents' point of view, the direction of fit depends on the direction of connections between the mind and the world. Thus, beliefs go from the *mind-to-world*; desires and intentions go in the opposite direction, from *world-to-mind*. The direction of adjustment makes it possible to explain the notion of "conditions of satisfaction." In the case of intentions, they are satisfied only if they are carried out; wishes are fulfilled, and beliefs are

[18] Not all consciousness is intentional, and not all intentionality is conscious.

confirmed if things are as I think they are. Thus, the fundamental intentional states are belief and desire (Searle, 1983, p. 28). Belief-related states include certainty, anticipation, expectation, and supposition, whereas desire-related states encompass wanting, longing, craving, and yearning – each varying in intensity. In formal terms, intentional states are typically expressed by propositional attitudes of the form "believes that p" and "desires that p." These states are intrinsically linked to both perception and action, insofar as they mediate the organism's cognitive engagement with the world and its motivational orientation toward it. However, intentionality alone is not enough to explain human action; it is necessary to consider *intention-in-action*. Searle has stressed the gap between intentional states and action (see Searle, 2001, p. 144). There is here a close similitude to Marshall's (1868) argument in *Ye Machine*.

In most economic theories, intentionality is missing when explaining economic activity. Contrary to mainstream economics, a system approach leaves room for intentional categories of action. Thus, in evolutionary economics, intentionality is significant because it emphasizes that economic change is not purely mechanistic or externally imposed but is driven by agents' purposeful actions and decisions. Agents have goals, preferences, and strategies that influence their behavior and, consequently, the broader economic system. The interaction of these intentional actions forms a foundational aspect of economic evolution. Felin and Foss (2009, p. 164) have recognized that intentionality deserves more attention in future work in this area because "individuals within organizations have intentions, beliefs, interests, and expectations that drive their behavior in collective settings." In Section 3, we introduce the action plan approach, show how action plans embody intentionality, and explain how our approach bridges intentionality and economics.

3 Action Plans

3.1 Elements and Morphology of Action Plans

The formation of plans is a central activity in the general processes of the interactive deployment of human action.[19] The result of planning is bundles of alternative action plans or courses of action that the agent perceives as possible. Plans link together the goals or objectives (ends) of action, which are, in turn, connected in the agent's mind with possible (imagined) future states valued as more desirable, and the sequences of actions (which include the provision of means) to achieve those goals. From this perspective, action plans can be

[19] Although not all intentional action is planned and conscious (e.g., an emotional reaction), this is a way of articulating a systematic exposition of the role of intentionality in explaining evolutionary phenomena resulting from human action.

analyzed as systems composed of goals, actions, and connective relationships. Intentionality determines the direction of those actions. Thus, action plans form a basic structure that, incorporating intentionality, articulates actions, goals, and selection between alternatives, serves as a guide to act, control action, and evaluate the performance of human action deployed in interaction.

The Austrian school of economics followers have especially highlighted this way of thinking about action in economics, but not only they.[20] However, sometimes, mentioning the concept of plan leads some to confuse planning with centralized planning, a main characteristic of command economies, but this is not the case.[21] Individuals, in a more or less lax or rigorous way, plan their vacations, studies, or how to take advantage of investment opportunities. The same is true for organizations, such as firms, which must design and execute business plans that include investment, human resource management, financing, and marketing plans. Obviously, a command economy has very different properties from economies in which rival plans are continually being launched into a competitive environment (see Tinbergen, 1961).

In abstract terms, each set of elements and connections characterizes the topology and properties of a system. Evolutionary processes are put into motion mainly through recombining connections among given elements and introducing new elements together with new connections. These new combinations give rise to new interactions and emergent properties that may generate novelties, which may be intended or not. An action plan is a quasi-decomposable system that is formed with, and embedded in, other systems of different nature, such as organizations, institutions, physical and social systems, with which it interacts.

The very nature of an action plan is systemic. It consists of a projected sequence of actions toward goals. This structure can be represented in a simple way. In Figure 2, we depict two simple action plans. On the left, we have a plan that unfolds in three periods. First, at time t, two actions are deployed $(a_1,\ a_2)$. In the next period $(t+1)$, an intermediate goal (O_1) is reached and a new action (a_3) is executed to reach at period $t+2$ the final goal (O_2) that gives the direction and sense of the whole plan. For example, I plan to fly from Los

20 Of course, the concept of action plans is not new in economics. It can be found in economists of quite different traditions, such as Keynes (1936), Hicks (1939), Stackelberg (1946 [1943]), Eucken (1940), Debreu (1959), Lachmann (1977), Malinvaud (1999), Boulding (1991), Metcalfe (2004), Rubio de Urquía (2005), Wagner (2012). For authors like Debreu, plans are merely a label. For others, like Eucken, Rubio de Urquía, and Wagner, it is a central pillar of their theories. More recently, the definition of objectives and plans is a fundamental part of the so-called agent-based models (Tesfatsion, 2021).

21 According to Hayek (1945, p. 520), the question of how to organize economic activity "is not a dispute about whether planning is to be done or not. It is a dispute about whether planning is to be done centrally . . . or is to be divided among many individuals."

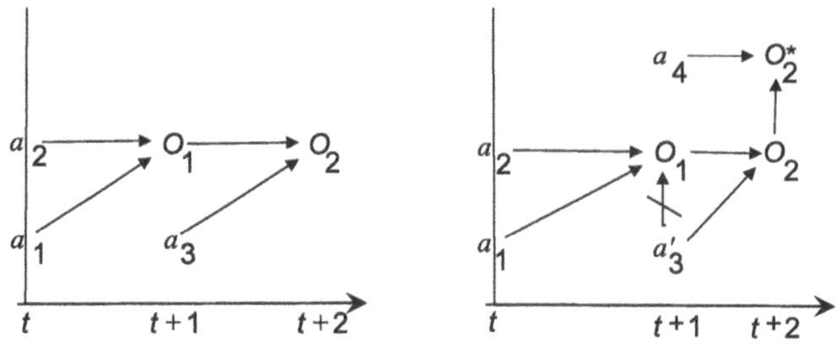

Figure 2 Examples of graphical representations of action plans.
Source: Encinar and Muñoz (2006, p. 265).

Angeles to Madrid tomorrow. First, I have to book a flight and pay for it (actions 1 and 2) today to have the flight (goal 1) tomorrow. The next day, I go to the airport and board the plane (action 3) to fly to Madrid, where I arrive the following day (goal 2). On the right, there is a more complex plan that incorporates four actions and a new goal (O_2^*) that is hierarchically dominant of the intermediate goal O_2 and a crossed arrow that means that action a_3' does not produce the (intermediate) goal O_1 – that is, this represents a kind of logical or material impossibility.[22] These graphic structures allow two essential elements to be highlighted. On the one hand, they show the "topology" of the plan, its shape, and its logical and hierarchical structure. On the other hand, they show the plan's systemic nature and its projective nature toward the future.

In general, plans are integrated into other plans. They are usually subsystems of other, more general plans of the same agent (such as developing a *lifestyle*) or of other agents (contributing to the development of a product, founding a company with other partners, participating in social life (political and economic). Thus, a personal plan can be linked to objectives or organically depend on the objectives or actions of another agent – for example, my travel plans must be integrated into the plans of an airline. Therefore, the plans must be partially compatible with those of other agents. Of course, plans usually rival one another for execution, need scarce resources, and come into blatant conflict with the plans of others. The compatibility of plans – not only their contents but also their time horizons – is necessary for cooperation. Thus, the coordination of productive or exchange activities is essential for the functioning of a relatively complex society. On the other hand, plans may pursue objectives or require actions and resources that conflict with the plans of other agents. A less developed topic in

[22] An example of action 3 that does not produce the effect in this case is that on the day I have to fly to Madrid, there is a strike by pilots. An example of a superior objective is that the main goal is not to arrive in Madrid, but to do so to attend a very important business meeting (goal O_2^*). Thus, the only way to attend the meeting is via Zoom (action 4).

economics concerns the internal properties of action plans: their logical compatibilities, material consistency, ex ante compatibility with the plans of other agents, and so on.[23]

Departing from the concept of an action plan, Economic Theory can be understood as the study of how and why economic agents who interact in an environment form and adopt some action plans (and no others), and which outcomes result from the interactive deployment of such plans, which include changes in the agents and the socioeconomic environment. For the sake of simplicity, we will assume henceforth that agents adopt only one plan at each instant of time. However, in general, agents usually deploy two or more plans simultaneously – for example, flying to Madrid and finishing reading a book.

3.2 Plans and the Space of Representations

At each instant of time and for each agent, the agents ($i = 1, 2, \ldots \; N_t$) that populate the economy: (1) *form* bundles of alternative courses of action $\left(B_t^i\right)$; (2) *adopt*, within those bundles, the courses of action (plans) that they want to make effective because they consider them, according to their subjective criteria, as the best options in the decision context $\left(\bar{p}_t^i\right)$, where $\left(\bar{p}_t^i \in B_t^i\right)$; (3) attempt to deploy, in interaction with other agents and the physical and social milieu the sequences of actions envisaged in those plans to attain the expected goals; and (4) *evaluate* the performance (apply the conditions of satisfaction) of their plans and revise the plans within the bundle of plans, and eventually form completely new bundles of plans $\left(B_{t+1}^i\right)$. This evolving sequence is represented in Figure 3.

A key question is, where do plans come from? According to Miller et al. (1960, p. 177ff), plans usually come from old plans, from old courses of action that have proven, at least to an extent, to be successful enough. These authors also add other layers that they call meta plans – plans to generate plans – heuristic plans (1960, p. 179), and so on. In a popular text, Pólya (1945) distinguishes four phases in the heuristic process: we (as any other scientist) (1) understand the problem; (2) devise a plan that will guide the solution and connect the data to the unknown – this implies creativity –; (3) carry out our plan of the solution, checking each step as we go; and (4) look back at the completed solution, reviewing, checking, discussing, perhaps even improving it. This is a typical, if somewhat linear, sequence for a scientist, as we have assumed for our economic agent operating under uncertainty. Of course, in reality, there are more backward and forward movements between these phases. When we cannot solve a problem, we have to consider some similar problems, and we can

[23] A systematic treatment of consistency and unfeasibility of action plans is Encinar (2002).

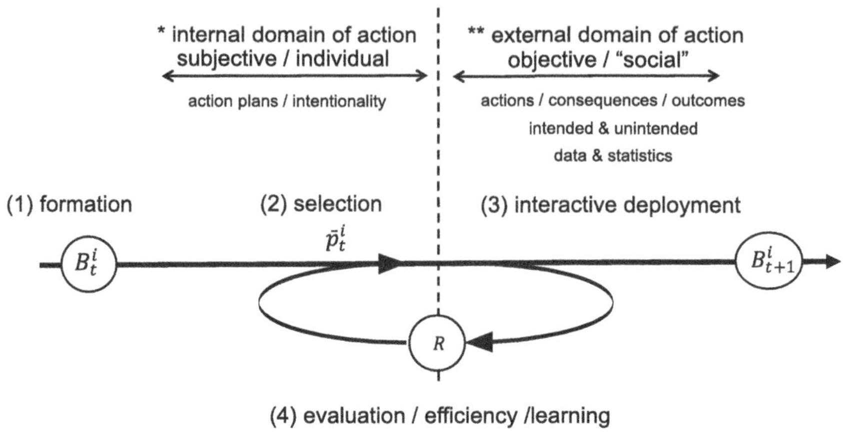

Figure 3 The evolving sequence of action plans. Source: Muñoz and Encinar (2019, p. 927). B_t^i refers to the bundle of plans at t by agent i, and $\overline{p}_t^i$ to the selected plan.

also work backwards. In Pólya's (1945, p. 181) words, "What is the situation we are trying to reach?"

How can we connect this kind of argument with intentionality? First, we should examine how agents form their plans and what the inputs are to *produce* them. When forming their bundles of action plans, agents, departing from their intentional states, determine what they *believe* they can do, what they *wish* to do, and *how to proceed* in a social context. Of course, those sequences of actions and goals included in plans are imagined and deemed possible (Shackle, 1979, p. 26) by agents. Thus, the formation of personal action plans depends on the agents' particular sets of personal characteristics; for example, their internal structures of beliefs, attitudes, values, and theoretical and practical representations of reality. These sets of characteristics may be analyzed if we write them down as sets of statements about what each individual perceives as existing, based on what he or she knows, feels, and wants. Rubio de Urquía (2005) has referred to this structure as the *personal ensemble*.[24] Personal ensembles are idiosyncratic and critical in understanding the connections of individuals' plans with culture, values, technology, and society in which they interact. First, the ensembles depend on the agent's cognitive and ethical dynamics and the cultural environment. Second,

[24] Rather similar notions are *constructs* (Kelly, 1955), *shared mental models* (Denzau & North, 1994), *space of representations* (Loasby, 1999), and *personal agency beliefs* (Harper, 2003). Although we refer here to persons or individuals, these ensembles can also be predicated on organizations: they include the organization's culture, values, knowledge base, strategy, and vision.

economic processes ignite when agents select which courses of action they will attempt to unfold. The way they value different alternative plans and the likelihoods they assign to each are subjective. In any case, once a decision is made, each agent undertakes the *external actions* (Figure 1) following the action plan in an attempt to transform the physical and social reality in which they live according to their intended goals. Finally, agents evaluate what is being produced (reached) according to their sequences of planned goals. As far as what is being executed and achieved conforms to what was previously planned, they would judge whether their action is efficient (see below). Deviations (partial success or complete failure) from planned sequences of actions and pursued goals would eventually determine adjustments to the action plans, including the revision of actions, goals, and connections, and even the total removal of plans.

A bundle of plans of action in a neoclassical account would roughly correspond to a firm's production set or the consumer's affordable consumption set. Over these sets, an objective function (such as profits or utility) is defined, and according to the principle of economic behavior, the agent chooses the production plan or consumption vector that maximizes profit or utility. However, in a more general and realistic situation, where partial knowledge and genuine uncertainty prevail, agents choose bundles that would "meet targets of adequacy rather than pinnacles of attainment" (Earl, 1983, pp. 78–81). In a somewhat similar vein, Earl (1983, pp. 149–150) discusses a multistage process in which agents proceed following the sequence: (1) problem recognition (a failure to match up to aspirations); (2) search of (not given) courses of action; (3) evaluation of possible sequels of particular choices; (4) choice itself; (5) implementation (often challenging and partially accomplished); and (6) assessment (the agent examines to which extent what was decided was achieved). For Potts (2000, pp. 120–123), agents form conjectures as a solution by means of searching among adjacent possibilities, among which may be found a more promising way of solving their particular problems. In this case, the "decision cycle" that makes these operations possible consists of four separate components: LIST, CONSTRUCT, RANK, SELECT.

The ensembles refer to the "reality" as it is conceived by the agents and produce their spaces of representation. Agents use their cultural and individual matrices of beliefs, values, attitudes, and even emotions, to form plans of action – conjectures on how to transform reality. In our approach, "beliefs" refers to the set of conceptions, representations, and knowledge to which the individual is faithful. In general, beliefs imply evaluation criteria that organize projective action and the action of decision among alternatives and value judgments. "Values" is the set of valuation criteria effectively used by the individual to organize the action and issue value judgments projectively. In the terminology of the intentionality literature, we have beliefs and desires, along with their corresponding conditions of satisfaction. Thus, the possible difference between the valuation criteria implied by the beliefs and those effectively used in practice must be acknowledged. Values include tastes and preferences.[25] "Attitudes" refers to stable features that introduce determination in certain aspects.[26] These elements configure the intentional states and intentionality of action plans.

It is through the simultaneous carrying out of plans in interdependent contexts that planning connects to observable action. It is at this stage that, on the one hand, intentionality emerges and produces external reality, and, on the other, it is possible to show the analytical link between the micro- (individual) and meso-level. This is the crucial stage in which action is deployed interactively, producing instants of reality and the historical consequences of action – those captured in ordinary statistical measures, and so on. Interaction reveals which parts of the plans of interacting agents within a system are or are not compatible, and it retains ex post which parts of goals and courses of action considered ex ante as possible have been successful. In other words, agents examine whether their conjecture (the bundle of plans) was correct and whether their goals have been attained. If evidence is unsatisfactory, agents would revise how they form their plans to try to do so otherwise. Thus, as long as plans are being developed, they are evaluated, and learning processes are triggered. Interaction initiates a selection process external to the agent.

Kelly (1955 [1963]), like Hayek (1952), stressed the human ability to generalize and use analogy: Humans are good at imposing patterns on their surrounding world. Thus, pattern matching is how we perceive, remember, and comprehend reality. On this basis, humans can be seen as *scientists* who construct theories (*conjectures*) about how the physical and social world works in the face of uncertainty. Action plans are conjectures. According to Koppl (2002, p. 107), "The point of our plans is precisely to change events, to move

[25] In our approach, preferences play a very important but subordinate role compared to their role in mainstream economics. In the latter case, preferences are a primary input to decision theory, usually taken as given, as in microeconomics. On the contrary, our approach implies a potentially broader treatment of preferences, because it links their location within a theory of action to the question of their origin and evolution. An evolutionary account of evolutionary preferences can be found in Earl (2022), chapter 7. See also Bianchi (1998).

[26] These two dynamics are supported by the transformation of the systems of higher order, for example, the institutional and cultural systems, to which agents belong, including the natural and the social environment. For more details, see Cañibano et al. (2017).

them from the path they would otherwise take." Agents make plans only in the field of action or part of the world they think they can control (at least to some degree), giving them "enough subjective predictability to expect the desired result with the required degree of confidence. That field of action is filled with hypothetical propositions of the type: 'If I do this, that follows.'" (2002, p. 107) Expectations integrate into the action plans of agents, setting and shaping the goals of action as desired future states of the system and the sequence of actions to produce them. Thus, agents' plans can also be conceived as experiments based on conjectural knowledge to coordinate their activities with other agents. Available scientific and tacit knowledge, as well as the evolution of technology, raise expectations about new niches of opportunities related to both ends and means.

Expectations can evolve, affecting the formulation of plans and the actions agents deploy. Concerning the future, under this approach, imagination and creativity play key roles (Koppl et al., 2015; Lewis, 2017). Agents also use (develop and adapt) conventions (Keynes, 1936), routines, institutions, and technologies to manage uncertainty (Loasby, 1999). Besides conjectural knowledge (Loasby, 1984; Popper, 1972), other elements concur in explaining economic change. For instance, the dynamics of goal setting, the hierarchical rearrangement, and the eventual removal of action goals, as well as the intentionality of the agents (Muñoz et al., 2011).

As shown below, economic dynamics can be understood as the process of generating, selecting, and attempting to implement agents' action plans and their consequences. The alteration of intentionality implies that agents' action plans are internally modified in the spaces of representation and that the interactive implementation of the new plans generates new realities. Indeed, introducing new objectives alters the spaces of representation and induces new knowledge, goals, capabilities, and plans.

3.3 Rules, Routines, Capabilities, and Plans

Although the projective and intentional dimensions of action plans provide them with their essential nature, a large part of action plans are generally formed by reusing parts of old plans or complete plans that have proven to be especially successful (effective) in producing the desired effects (changes) in the world. In this way, many of the actions of agents are routinized and based on rules, economizing mainly cognitive resources. Action plans integrate rules, routines, and exploit capabilities. The agents can apply the resources and mental energies thus economized to explore and experiment with new conjectures and achieve new goals.

In the context of evolutionary economics, rules are fundamental to understanding the structure and dynamics of both individual behavior and institutional evolution. Philosophically, and in the context of intentionality, Searle (1995) has distinguished between *regulative rules*, which govern existing forms of behavior (e.g., traffic laws), and *constitutive rules*, which create the very possibility of certain social practices (e.g., "X counts as Y in context C," such as money or property rights). Constitutive rules are crucial in economics because they underpin the institutional facts that make markets, firms, and contracts intelligible and functional. According to Searle, such rules are not externally imposed constraints but part of the social ontology that enables collective intentionality and coordinated action. On his part, Douglas North (1990, 2005), conceptualizes institutions as "humanly devised constraints that structure political, economic, and social interaction," distinguishing between *formal rules* (laws, constitutions, and property rights) and *informal norms* (customs, conventions, and social codes). North emphasizes that institutions evolve incrementally and path-dependently, shaping the incentive structures within which agents operate. In evolutionary economics, these rules are not viewed as static constraints but rather as part of a coevolutionary process with technology, organizational routines, and beliefs (see Muñoz, 2024). Rules influence the formation and replication of routines, while adaptive pressures can lead to institutional change when existing rules become misaligned with evolving economic conditions.

In evolutionary economics, Nelson and Winter (1982) highlighted the concept of routines (see Becker, 2004) within firms as intentional strategies that evolve over time. The emergence and evolution of routines may be driven by routine recombination, as in Pentland et al. (2012), who propose a generative model of organizational routines and their change over time. As articulated by Nelson and Winter, routines function as the "genes" of firms, encoding organizational knowledge and enabling consistent responses to recurring problems. These routines encompass production methods, hiring practices, quality control procedures, and other rule-based activities that firms replicate over time. Routines reduce the need for constant deliberation and economize on bounded cognitive resources, providing firms and individuals with a stable platform for operating under uncertainty. In the case of firms, they aim to maintain or improve their competitive positions through various combinations of routines, thereby achieving differential growth and success (or failure) within industries.

The concept of routines is closely linked to the concept of capabilities. Whereas routines refer to specific, replicable patterns of action, capabilities denote a firm's capacity to deploy and reconfigure those routines to achieve strategic objectives (Teece et al., 1997). In this sense, dynamic capabilities – those that enable firms to adapt, innovate, and renew their resource base – are seen as higher-order routines that guide organizational change. Evolutionary economists emphasize that capabilities and routines are developed historically through path-dependent processes, influenced by organizational learning, past investments, and institutional context.[27]

Rather than being driven purely by exogenous shocks or optimal investment strategies, innovation emerges from internal experimentation, market selection feedback, and interfirm imitation. Some routines prove more adaptive than others, leading to differential firm performance and, ultimately, evolutionary selection at the industry level. This approach provides a rich explanation for technological diversity, persistent heterogeneity among firms, and the cumulative, nonlinear nature of economic change.

Loasby (1998, 1999) analyzes this concept by relating it to the limitations and potential of human cognition, especially in terms of the connections between intelligence and action.[28] In his view, capabilities are endogenous and idiosyncratic, as their development is influenced by the context and by how individuals interpret it, guided by the institutional framework provided by formal and informal organizations. In a context of genuine uncertainty, conjectural knowledge may refer to knowledge of facts ("knowing that") – that may be subdivided into "knowing what" and "knowing why" – and that is, the ability to perform the appropriate actions to achieve a desired outcome ("knowing how"). Additionally, "knowledge how" may be direct and indirect and "includes skill both in performance and in recognizing when and where this skillful performance is appropriate" (Loasby, 1999, p. 51). In any case, all four kinds of knowledge are acquired by trial and error through "experiments" which may be carefully designed, as in the case of scientific knowledge, fairly casual, or often controlled by the unconscious processes of our brain.

Earl and Muñoz (2027a) describe the relationship between capabilities and routines. "Knowledge how" is mostly tacit, poorly articulated, and controlled in parts of the brain that developed prior to consciousness. This tacit knowledge encompasses some of the most effective skills, indicating the quality that unconscious coding systems can attain. One effective way of coding know-how is through habits and routines. "Routines are representations within the brain, and definitions of routines, even in the form of standard operating procedures, are public representations which are constrained by language and the concepts available." (Loasby, 1999, p. 64) Routines reduce cognition costs and

[27] Innovation, within this framework, is often the result of incremental modifications to existing routines or the recombination of routines in novel ways.

[28] For Loasby (1999, p. 49), the evolution of capabilities is a necessary element in any theory of economic change.

save time by imposing closure to situations that are too demanding of cognitive resources. Routine might seem to denote the absence of change, but all change requires substantial elements of stability. Routines provide stable patterns on which selection processes can operate, and the stable patterns of individual and subunit behavior, which permit the development of indirect capabilities that impose coherence on an organization's activities.

Rules may be thought of as routines and may similarly be divided into the prescriptive and the procedural (Loasby, 1999, p. 65). A particular virtue in an interdependent society is that widely shared rules help each of us predict others' behavior, enabling us to interact effectively and avoid conflict. Nevertheless, the process of explicitly codifying routines may help clarify both the routine and its domain, thereby defining and limiting closure and raising the performance of those whose tacit knowledge within the relevant field is well below the standard of experts.

Like other institutions and rules, capabilities economize on individual cognition and increase the compatibility of thought and action between those who use the same categories and procedures. Hayek's view was that the best general rules were those that had survived the testing of many generations and had been incorporated into the cognitive systems of vast numbers of people. Rules and routines, most of which are not clearly defined or even explicitly stated, provide an institutional setting for each individual's use of knowledge.

3.4 Intentionality and Rationality

A central concept in economics is rationality. Although, for reasons of space and the complexity of this topic, we cannot delve into it here to the depth it deserves, we must address rationality in the context of intentionality and action plans. Intuitively, by rational behavior, we can understand behavior according to reasons to act (Searle, 2001). On the other hand, rationality suggests proportionality between, again in our case, what is desired to be done and the means that are needed or at the disposal of agents to be deployed to achieve the objectives of the action. In the latter case, rationality would allude to its etymological meaning (*ratio* in Latin). However, many versions or conceptions of rationality are not necessarily convergent. For example, Max Weber distinguished four types of motives guiding social actions: instrumentally rational, value rational, affectual, and traditional (see Crespo, 2013, p. 762). For his part, Peter Earl (2022), echoing Simon, distinguishes between procedural and substantive rationality. A decision is substantively rational if judged to be the best possible choice regarding its outcomes, given a set of alternatives and a specific goal. It assumes full knowledge of all relevant options, consequences, and a well-ordered preference system. This is the form of rationality assumed in neoclassical economics and optimization models. On the contrary, a decision is procedurally rational if it is made through a reasonable process, using limited information and bounded cognitive capacities, even if the outcome is not the absolute best. The emphasis is on how decisions are made, not just on the decision itself, and reflects human cognitive limitations (Simon's bounded rationality). While substantive rationality is often unrealistic in real-world decision-making because it presupposes omniscience and unlimited cognitive resources, processual (procedural) rationality values satisficing (choosing an option that is good enough) rather than maximizing utility. If economics is a process, the decision is a process, and action is a process, rationality should be procedural. Finally, Sugden (1991, 2005) introduces a critical discussion between the positive (descriptive) and normative aspects of rationality, distinguishing instrumental rationality, ultimately based on Hume's position, and more modern ones (such as that of Savage, von Neumann, and game theory) that insist on the consistency of choices.[29]

Which of these versions would best suit our overall action plan approach? For sure, an axiomatic version of rationality (like substantial rationality) that not only excludes the possibility of "irrational" behavior but also claims complete knowledge is at odds with our approach. We must discard this alternative. Additionally, we must be aware of the risk that, according to Shackle (1972, pp. 443–444), resides in what, by its nature, it is obliged to neglect or even implicitly declare unimportant imagination, the source of novelty. One proposal is to employ an instrumental version of rationality in a dynamic context. According to this, human reason would operate on the material provided by the acting agents' beliefs, knowledge, and values (eventually also the emotions).[30] As we have seen before, these elements are the sources of the cognitive and ethical dynamics that, together with the cultural dynamics of society, form the bundles of action plans among which agents choose. Thus, rationality is linked, through action plans, to intention: as far as intentionality is the tendency toward a goal that first appears in the individual's mind as a purpose, intention is the determination of will in accordance with a purpose instantiated in a plan. Intentionality provides direction, guidance, and rationality to action. Any change in the intentionality of an action plan modifies its

[29] An interesting discussion about rationality in the social world is Schutz (1943). See also Rizzo (2015).

[30] Like ours, Hume's instrumental rationality is based on a theory of causal relationships between mental states (ideas and impressions). The relationships that Hume postulates are liable to induce various forms of nonrational behavior, some of which have since been observed in controlled experiments. (Sugden, 2005, p. 115)

structure, content, and/or goals – or the hierarchy of goals – and has consequences at the micro and meso levels of interaction and even modifies, if they spread enough, the behavior and properties of the whole system (macro level). The fact that unexpected events arise from the interaction of intentional dynamics does not eliminate the fact that their origin is intentional. Purpose activates behavior and actions that focus on their achievement through intention and will. Agents can be distinguished not only because of their knowledge and skills but also by the purposes they pursue. All this leads to considering agents that can introduce a wide variety of changes in their (local) environments through their actions, altering other agents' space of action.

3.5 Plans and Microlevel Efficiency

States and intentional actions incorporate conditions of satisfaction. The equivalent concept in economics is that of efficiency. Efficiency is another core concept in economics. In mainstream economics, efficiency typically refers to a situation in which all available resources are allocated in a manner that maximizes total social welfare, *given* existing technology and preferences. The concept of efficiency typically includes allocative efficiency (as is the case with Pareto (1909) efficiency), productive efficiency, and dynamic efficiency (Huerta de Soto, 2009). Moreover, efficiency is associated with equilibrium. For example, commenting on Hahn's (1974) definition of equilibrium in terms assesses that it is not an equilibrium of prices and quantities but of theory and policy – the equivalent to action plans. As such, an agent's theory is "a procedure for deriving predictions (which may take the form of a probability distribution) from information; his policy is a procedure for deriving decisions from predictions. ... Professor Hahn offers the following definition (1974, p. 25): 'an economy is in equilibrium when it generates messages which do not cause agents to change the theories which they hold or the policies which they pursue'. ... " (Loasby, 1983, pp. 104–105). A similar claim to Hayek's (1937) concept of equilibrium as the compatibility of agents' action plans. In this case, time plays a crucial role.

However, in an evolutionary context, where future events are unknown and mostly imagined, efficiency raises several issues linking intended action to actual action. As shown previously, the interactive deployment of the adopted courses of action produces the different products of action (goods, services, relationships, etc.) that are registered in statistical and historical records. The comparison of the expected sequence of outcomes considered in deployed action plans with what is being achieved leads economic agents to continuously evaluate their plans, introducing changes in them, eventually forming new plans of action – reconfiguring the bundles of action plans – and producing new instants of reality, and so on. Under uncertainty, efficiency refers to actions deployed within an evolving, complex system rather than just to *choices* in a given situation. In this sense, "deployed action is efficient if it *produces* the projected goals of action" (Muñoz & Encinar, 2019, p. 921). In other words, efficiency refers to the adequacy of connections between actions and goals, ensuring that agents' intentions produce facts and states of affairs as expected when action plans are formed.

Economic efficiency is a systemic property, but it can also be applied to individual actions at the micro level. Thus, there is evolutionary efficiency *at the micro level* when an agent's updated intentions result in the projected goals being achieved in action plans. Of course, the state of the system within which agents interact is not independent of their actions; however, the outcome of those actions is determined through an intricate and complex system of interactions that unfolds over historical time. Individual and collective intentionality of action (Tomasello et al., 2005) are linked to expectations. As a result, the concept of expectations binds the theory of action to efficiency. Efficiency of action – at the micro level – should be judged in terms of a more or less permanent/recurrent mismatch between what agents intentionally pursue and what they reach due to the interactive deployment of their action, that is, the mismatch between planned and actual action.[31] To accommodate efficiency in our approach, we need to depart from the difference between the expected (and judged possible) outcome and the effective outcome,[32] resulting from the interaction of agents' action plans.

The expectation of agent i about his state of the system at $t + 1$ – his "state of expectations" – expresses a desire: What is expected and, in some sense, what the agent wants to reach. Thus, expectation incorporates the intentionality of the agent. When differences between what is observed by an agent and what is expected are considered significant in some subjective sense, agents trigger processes of learning: Agents will attempt to remove or reduce the sources of their rationed action. They will look for and eventually identify the sources and nature of the obstacles that prevent them from successfully achieving their goals of action.[33] This process of checking conjectures usually implies the need to change theories and beliefs about reality. Agents might be able to

[31] However, in genuine dynamic processes, we should expect divergence between the expected and what is actually obtained.

[32] "How effective" is not real in the sense of *external*, something that is there, but what the agent perceives as real.

[33] This is a rather stylized argument. Of course, agents often cannot repeat or experiment with actions to determine the source of failure, nor can the context be repeated.

identify obstacles in the social environment of interaction (external domain of action) – for example, the existence of conflicting goals – or within their own dynamics of generating intentional action (internal domain). We say "might be able" because a priori, there is no guarantee that agents will be able to do so. In a negative sense, the (degree of) failure to fulfill the plans is a measure of the inefficiency of action. We assume that, to some extent, agents can interpret and determine why their plans failed; however, we are aware that the Duhem–Quine thesis suggests that it can be very challenging to know why a plan failed within a complex system. Agents will review parts or the whole bundle of action plans if they judge that those plans are not being effective enough. Accordingly, agents can establish or explore new connections, which will trigger renewed processes of learning and experimentation as they explore adjacent states within the system in which they interact.

Conflict and error play an important role in our approach. The differences between the desired and pursued state and what was achieved by agents may have different reasons. For example, they may arise because expectations are poorly formed; due to lack of knowledge (Hayek, 1937; Kirzner, 1992; Loasby, 1999; Simon, 1983); the presence of inconsistencies in goals (Sen, 1993); the absence of appropriate learning mechanisms – and even negative learning (Almudí et al., 2016); and so on. In the process of deployment of actual action, elements of "irrationality" may appear linked, for example, to states of mood, physical and psychological factors, emotions, luck, blows of fate, and so on. Moreover, social dynamics of interaction (mainly culture and institutions) can promote, limit, or even cancel specific courses of action that ex ante would appear perfectly feasible and consistent, that, when deployed, may collide with the action deployed by other agents, returning *ex post* rationed action.

4 Interaction

4.1 The Emergence of Novelties and Complexity

Socioeconomic processes are a distinct type of process that unfold over historical time. The interactive deployment of agents' plans of action configures the socioeconomic processes, which, in turn, create new possibilities of action for people and societies. The interaction of renewed action plans constitutes the basis of the evolution of complex evolutionary socioeconomic systems (Muñoz et al., 2011). The outcomes of economic processes appear in many different forms (production of goods and services, consumption, investment in physical and human capital, exchange and trade, rules, organizations, institutions, etc.). These outcomes – recorded in statistics, organizational forms, physical and social technologies – are the consequences of human interaction.

Emergence is a key concept for explaining economic change. Usually, emergence is connected to innovations or the appearance of novelties. There are two primary sources of novelties: interaction and recombination. Novelty due to new combinations is a central theme of Schumpeterian and evolutionary economics (Antonelli & Colombelli, 2025; Loasby, 2007). For example, action plans, which form network structures of actions and goals, are structures themselves that are continuously changing because individuals and expectations change, and because of reflexivity (see Section 5.1; Beinhocker, 2013; Soros, 2013). It is over the renewed variety of connections embedded in plans that selection and retention mechanisms operate. All this happens at the micro level. At a meso level, the interaction of purposeful action gives rise to systems and subsystems – such as machines, computers, the Internet, routines, rules, institutions, and informal norms – that emerge. Structural change and the emergence of new properties – including technologies, institutions, rules, and markets – are the consequence of recombining different links among these systems. Experimental tinkering (Koppl et al., 2019) is essential in making connections. From within, actors recombine the different elements of the subsystems – mainly plans – according to their expectations and the evaluation they attach to the "observed" outcomes of interaction. Recombining connections is a particularly appropriate method for processes that require experimentation. Trial and error are typically guided by conjectures intended to produce particular results, although most conjectures are refuted, and unintended consequences are relatively common.[34] Path dependence is another common feature of complex systems. Once put into motion, the evolving system – the economy, the sector, the industry, the firm – generates new knowledge, artifacts, and sets of rules that undermine some established knowledge while also supplying the elements for further innovation in a creatively destructive process.

The emergence of complexity within an economic system is not necessarily intentional. However, it depends on the agents' intentional behavior, even though what happens is not necessarily what the agents seek. Observed actions can differ from what was intentionally sought – when they still were projected actions – although this is compatible with intentionality in the analytical structure of action. The question about where and when new properties emerge may be addressed as follows. New properties emerge because agents change or rearrange plans by: (a) discovering or inventing new courses of action; and/or (b) discovering or inventing new objectives; and/or (c) rearranging previously existing actions and goals in a *new* way. Agents implement all these new or

[34] However, to assess the effectiveness of such experiments, some conditions of stability are needed.

revised actions and/or goals into *new* plans and try to deploy such action plans in interaction with other agents and the external environment. Thus, revised actions consist of introducing entirely new actions linked to existing objectives (a radical understanding of novelty) or changing (or canceling) the links between actions and objectives. Revised objectives consist of introducing entirely new ones or changing the existing hierarchy of objectives. However, it is because of the simultaneous carrying out of actions in interdependent contexts that novelties finally emerge.

We can formally represent this analytical sequence of events. Consider the following elements:

(1) We depart from an initial situation or state of affairs for each agent, as they perceive it, at the initial instant of time t; we will denote this state by s_t^i.
(2) Agents interact within *external* socioeconomic and physical environment systems, the state of which we represent by u_t.
(3) The cognitive and ethical dynamics of agents, δ_t^i, "interpret" those states and reproduce the ensemble of agents, E_t^i.
(4) From their respective ensembles, each agent produces the corresponding bundles of action plans, $\hat{B}_t^i$.
(5) Finally, each agent *selects* – the operation of selection represented with the "function" $\alpha^i()$ – the plans that will try to deploy producing *actual actions*, A_t^i in the external reality of agents.[35]

In a more compact way, we can represent all these dynamics at each instant of time and for each agent by means of the following formalism:

$$s_t^i \rightarrow \delta^i\left(s_t^i, u_t\right) \rightarrow \left(E_t^i, \hat{B}_t^i\right) \rightarrow \alpha^i\left(\hat{B}_t^i\right) \rightarrow A_t^i = \left\{s_t^i, A_t^i\right\}$$

In this context, the emergence of novelties can be both (1) the result of an agent's internal dynamics $\delta^i\left(s_t^i, u_t\right)$ – that reproduce new E_t^i, $\hat{B}_t^i$ and A_t^i– and/or (2) the result of interaction processes – the consequences of the deployment of actions A_t^i – between agents. The former refers to conscious, intentional acts undertaken by agents, the latter primarily to unexpected products of interactions among action plans.

Hence, at the system level, we have that, for each agent $i = 1, 2, \ldots N_t$, the pair $\left\{s_t^i, A_t^i\right\}$ represents the state of the agent $\left(s_t^i\right)$, and the effectively deployed courses of action $\left(A_t^i\right)$ in interaction with the other agents of the socioeconomic system with which it interacts and with the physical–social environment. The general structure of agents' interaction and the evolution (which implies

[35] This "function" includes the effects of preferences and emotions on the selection of a particular course of action.

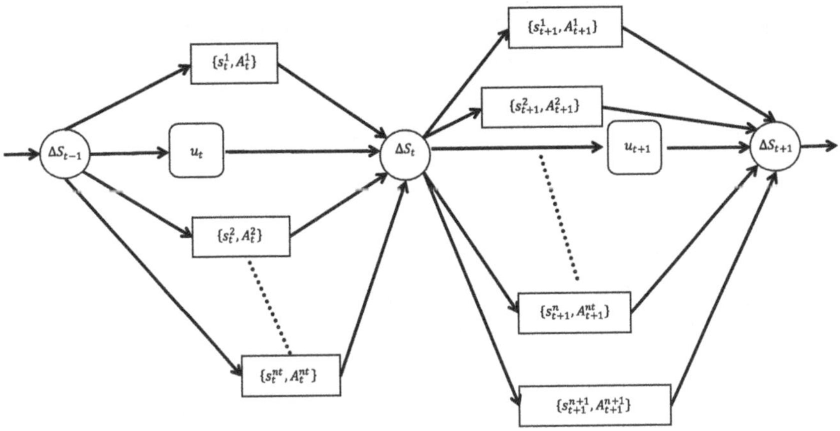

Figure 4 A representation of the structure of agent interaction and the evolution of socioeconomic systems. Observe that from t to $t + 1$ new agents may appear or existing ones disappear.

Source: Muñoz and Encinar (2014a, p. 329).

structural change) of the socioeconomic system (ΔS_t) over time $(t = 1, 2, \ldots T)$ can be depicted as in Figure 4.

The consequence of this interaction is a restless mechanism (à la Metcalfe) that generates continuous structural change. In the model, intentionality is located in the ensembles $\left(E_t^i\right)$ and deploys its logic through the interaction of the revised agents' plans. Revised action plans, in which novelty has already emerged, induce economic change, giving rise to processes of novelty-dissemination. Revised action plans are a source of complexity, as they contribute to the generation of the renewed variety characteristic of evolutionary processes. This schema represents the connections between the states of agents, the physical–social system, and the general social system, including emergent properties and orders. Interaction leads to the general dynamic of production of social and economic reality, and due to the appearance of all kinds of novelties – creative responses, unexpected consequences of actions, rationed action, positive or negative externalities, path-dependency – breaks down the sequences of the effective implementation of action plans, and triggers an out-of-equilibrium dynamics. This kind of dynamics does not lead to chaos but instead generates complexity in the system of interacting agents and the nonsocial medium. Thus, intentionality is a sufficient, not necessary, condition for the emergence of new properties within complex systems.

According to the responses, positive or negative feedback in terms of Miller and Page (2007), systems stabilize, increase, or decrease their degree of complexity. The logic of this entire interaction mesh is more evident in specific case studies. Moreover, this logic becomes more apparent when the level of analysis chosen by the theory falls between the micro–meso and meso–macro levels (Dopfer, 2011; Dopfer et al., 2004).

4.2 Entrepreneurship

Entrepreneurship perfectly illustrates the role of intentionality in structural change processes. For example, entrepreneurs play a major role in creating new combinations which have emergent properties – as the iPhone's functional properties – as part of their plans to make profits from filling gaps in the existing capital structure (see Harper & Endres, 2012, p. 352ff). Entrepreneurs deliberately seek to disrupt existing markets and create new value through innovative products or processes, contributing to economic dynamism. According to Baumol (1990, p. 897), entrepreneurs are "persons who are ingenious and creative in finding ways that add to their own wealth, power, and prestige," and entrepreneurship is "the activity of creating and implementing a new business plan" (Metcalfe, 2004, p. 158).[36] Because plans require resources for activation, the entrepreneur specializes in making judgmental decisions about allocating scarce resources (Casson, 1982, p. 151). For making plans, the entrepreneur connects different elements and subsystems (such as devices, routines, and other plans) in new and original ways; they are the constructors of connections (Earl, 2003).

Thanks to quasi-decomposability and modularity, it is possible to construct a higher-order level system from different subsystems through recombination. For that, those lower-order subsystems must be complementary for the higher-order system to work. Complementarity refers to a reconfiguration of what is connected to what and plays a prominent role in evolutionary processes. According to Dopfer et al. (2016), complementarity can take two distinct forms in evolutionary economic systems: downward and upward complementarity. Downward complementarity implies increasing specialization and the division of labor, and proceeds by division, differentiation, and reorganization. This is basically a Smithian process. On the contrary, upward complementarity, the discovery of emergent complementarity between extant or new components and products, proceeds by making new combinations or cross-fertilization among seemingly different inputs. This is an essentially Schumpeterian process (Dopfer et al., 2016, p. 755). From our system perspective, an economic system comprises complementary modules whose dynamics depend on the

[36] The quotation continues: "in many cases but not all cases reducible to the creation of a new business entity, the prototypical small firm."

predominant type of complementarities at work. For example, downward complementarity arises from ongoing modularization, which breaks an already existing whole into its constituent parts. This is a source of economizing gains, resulting from specialization at the level of the parts, which leads to greater efficiency at the level of the whole. Increasing variety at the modular level also drives increasing economic complexity at the level of substitute inputs. In contrast, upward complementarity involves the creation of new wholes from existing parts, recombining existing factors of production to generate new technologies, goods, and services that can lead to the emergence of new markets and industries. The emergence and coevolution of Internet-based technologies and AI are examples of upward complementarity.[37]

As said before, complementarities are mainly the outcome of a process of recombination and the emergence of new structures, put into motion by entrepreneurs with the purpose of introducing (testing) a new product or service that will be valued by potential customers (entrepreneurial conjecture). According to the distinction between downward and upward complementarity, it is possible to distinguish two basic entrepreneurship styles (Dopfer et al., 2016, p. 758). Attached to downward complementarity, we have agents alert to opportunities for personal gain that can be tapped by arbitraging hidden inefficiencies (entrepreneurship à la Kirzner). On the other hand, upward complementarity implies visionary agents that create novelty through forming new combinations (entrepreneurship à la Schumpeter). Entrepreneurship associated with upward complementarity can generate a new "meso trajectory," the actualization of a new set of rule-combinations (Blind, 2017). However, it also has a disruptive or destructive effect at the meso– macro level as existing meso-level structures of rules are recoordinated (Dopfer & Potts, 2008).

Evolution operates as a process of search algorithm – the familiar mechanism of variation, selection, and retention – through a combinatorial *design space*. Decomposability, modularity, and recombination can explain how the design space is formed in the minds of agents or the strategies of organizations. The size of a design space depends on the number of modules or dimensions on which the design can be varied, as well as the number of possible variants for each module or dimension. According to Beinhocker (2011), evolutionary search (experimental) algorithms applied to human social evolution produce three design spaces relevant to economic evolution: (1) physical technologies, that is, methods and designs for transforming matter, energy, and information from one state into another in pursuit of a goal (or goals); (2) social technologies, the methods and designs for organizing people in pursuit of a goal or goals,

[37] In the area of online education, several examples can be seen in Harper et al. (2021).

which include rules and institutions; and (3) business plans, a design space that binds physical and social technologies together in enterprises or projects that pursue economic goals – for example, increasing profits, cutting costs, increasing market share, and so on.[38] The evolution of socioeconomic systems is the outcome of a process of coevolutionary search through these three design spaces. Agents – mainly entrepreneurs, consumers, and governments – seek superior fitness levels on these "landscapes" (Kauffman, 1993). Fitness depends on *intentions* integrated into entrepreneurs' business plans. This view assigns a prominent role to entrepreneurs. As new physical and social technologies are discovered and developed through experimental tinkering, they are combined and recombined into new business plans, which are then transformed into firms. The working of those firms then alters the physical and social fitness functions, leading to changes in the business plan fitness function and so on, creating a coevolutionary process. In this context, the role of entrepreneurs can by no means be exaggerated.

4.3 "Ethical" Novelties

Novelties do not have to be only technological; they can be organizational, and so on. Among the various types of innovations, we can consider some particularly noteworthy ones that are closely tied to the dynamics of objectives. In subsection 3.2, we referred to the concept of ethical dynamics, which involves the agents' conceptions of what reality ought to be (Rubio de Urquía, 2005, p. 89). Ethical dynamics encompass personal and shared values, beliefs, and ethical considerations that influence goal setting and the prioritization of objectives. Ethical dynamics are responsible for the practical adoption of decisions regarding "ought to be," "want," and "prefer." The formation of moral judgment, the conception of life projects, of action objectives, and the formation of taste are "products" of ethical dynamics, but so are decisions such as whether to initiate such a type of learning, those of overcoming observed logical inconsistencies, and so on. The contents and hierarchies of agents' objectives are transformed, changed, and evolved due to these dynamics, along with the evolution of culture, which transforms the spaces of agents' representations and, therefore, the system for generating action plans. A new type of innovation, associated with ethical dynamics, must then be considered. We will refer to it as ethical innovation.

Ethical novelty is defined as the emergence of new goals or the reorganization of existing objectives within agents' action plans. It represents a shift in the

[38] Culture can be considered an additional design space. All these spaces of design coevolve in complex ways.

values or ethical considerations that drive an agent's behavior, prompting new courses of action that differ from previous ones.[39] Unlike cognitive dynamics, which deal with improved strategies or adaptations within existing frameworks, ethical novelty involves a more profound, often transformative change that reshapes the underlying purposes and priorities of economic actions, as Ghoshal (2005) has shown. An ethical novelty can occur when: an agent redefines what he or she believes to be important or desirable for his or her personal or professional life; a collective shift in societal or organizational values leads to changes in the action plans of a group or institution; economic and social goals evolve in response to ethical considerations such as sustainability, social equity, or moral commitments.

Considering this kind of novelty in economic analysis provides a richer understanding of how socioeconomic systems evolve. As agents redefine their objectives in light of new ethical insights – that may result from social or lobbying pressure or a change in cultural values – this can lead to structural changes in the economy. These changes would include shifts in market preferences, the emergence of new industries or sectors (e.g., green technology driven by environmental ethics), or the transformation of existing business models to align with new ethical standards. For example, a company might shift its business strategy to focus on sustainable practices due to a new ethical commitment to environmental stewardship, thereby sparking innovation and influencing competitors to follow suit. Additionally, consumers may adjust their purchasing behavior in response to evolving ethical beliefs, such as a preference for fair-trade products, which can create new market dynamics and opportunities for firms. On some occasions, we can find practices such as "green washing" deliberately misleading signals – where firms try to present themselves as environmentally conscious, but it is all for show.

Many of these changes are not just reactive but proactive, arising from agents' evolving understanding of what is right or desirable. This aspect of intentionality, shaped by ethical reflection and discourse, plays a critical role in guiding economic development. This perspective suggests that economic change is not solely a response to external shocks or cognitive learning but can also originate endogenously from within agents through shifts in their ethical frameworks. Such a view aligns with evolutionary economics, where change is understood as a dynamic, adaptive process driven by the interactions between

[39] Of course, the idea of ethical novelties is not new. For example, Godin refers to the religious origin of the term innovation – originally, an innovation was a heresy (see Godin, 2008, p. 24). Cañibano et al. (2006) argue that economics has traditionally focused on cognitive dynamics – how economic agents learn, adapt, and modify their behavior based on knowledge and perception of reality – overlooking the significant role of ethical dynamics.

various agents and influenced by their evolving goals and values. To sum up, the concept of ethical novelty complements the evolutionary economics perspective, which sees economic change as an ongoing process of adaptation, innovation, and selection. In this framework, the intentionality of agents and their capacity for innovation are crucial. Ethical novelty extends this view by highlighting that innovations are not just technical or cognitive but can also be rooted in changes to the ethical landscape. The evolution of the economic system is not just a product of external forces or cognitive adjustments, but a complex, evolving system influenced by the intentional, ethical behavior of its agents.

4.4 Institutions and Organizations

Institutions impose restrictions on behavior. However, these restrictions do not have to harm economic and social activity. Instead, institutions facilitate the coordination of interactions and mitigate uncertainty. Just as air resistance allows airplanes to fly, the existence of institutions (formal and informal) is a condition for agents to have a minimum level of stability to plan and deploy their intentionality in a context of uncertainty and partial knowledge.

Institutions are based on rules; nevertheless, they go beyond mere rule integration. Institutions also enable new opportunities that can be explored, incorporating them as means or goals into renewed action plans. For Hodgson (2006), institutions are systems of established and prevalent social rules. These rules structure social interactions and may be "broadly understood as a socially transmitted and customary normative injunction or immanently normative disposition, that in circumstances X do Y" where "do" means "this counts as," "take this to mean," "refrain from" and so on. In Searle's (1995, p. 9) terms, "when the procedure or practice of counting X as Y becomes regularized, it becomes a rule. And rules of the form X counts as Y in C are then constitutive of institutional structures." Then, an institution is any system of constitutive rules of the form X counts as Y in C. Once an institution becomes established, it provides a structure within which one can create institutional facts." According to Rosenbaum (2022), the importance of institutions is derived from the fact that some institutions can be described as enabling rules – that enable actors to do certain things, such as speaking a language or playing chess. In doing so, enabling rules arguably require complementary mental models that contain knowledge about the rules, the context in which they are applied, and how to use them effectively.[40] This is particularly important from a societal

[40] In his discussion on versions of the extended cognition approach, Frolov (2024) explains how socially extended cognition is based on cognitive institutions. On the epistemic function of

perspective. Searle's ontological approach and North's historical perspective provide a valuable framework for understanding how rules enable, constrain, and evolve alongside economic behavior. They help explain why institutional change is often slow and uneven, and why economic performance is deeply embedded in the quality and adaptability of a society's rule systems.

Institutions – as well as rules, norms, and routines (see Section 3.3) – are tremendously helpful for agents when dealing with uncertainty and knowledge problems. Partial and conjectural knowledge in a context of uncertainty implies exploring ways to organize both formal and informal processes. It is in this context that the importance of organizations and institutions arises. A key role of organizations and institutions is to guide evolution, and both emerge from evolutionary processes.[41] Mainstream economics typically does not pay special attention to the nature and emergence of organizations and institutions, often taking them for granted, for example, markets. However, upon closer examination, we can see that a significant portion of economic activity is devoted to creating and maintaining capabilities, organizations, and institutions.

The connection between organizations and knowledge is more straightforward.[42] A vast amount of knowledge has been developed, and its application in society depends on organizations. Formal or informal organizations are also created by forming selective connections between groups that interact within the organization or with other organizations. This is the case of a firm that structures interaction between its members and the interaction of its members with elements of its environment. These structures encourage the formation of connections between the ideas and skills of those who are organizationally linked, while discouraging the formation of connections between the ideas and skills of those who are organizationally separated (see Loasby, 2008, p. 6). However, organizations also integrate action plans, and thus the intentionality of agents who cooperate within them. Collective action allows cooperation in the economic sphere. It also "aggregates" the intentions of individual agents into *collective intentions*, so crucial in the actions of organizations.[43] For Penrose (1959), the key function of firms is to organize resources within an

institutions, see also Dekker and Remic (2025). In a somewhat parallel investigation, Loasby highlights institutions' crucial role in the growth of knowledge. Among them, the institution of science stands out (see Ziman, 1978, 2000).

41 In fact, capabilities may be regarded as particular kinds of institutions. However, the connection between capabilities and institutions is indirect, through organizations.

42 What follows in this subsection is an excerpt of Earl and Muñoz (2027b).

43 "Collective intentionality covers not only collective intentions but also such other forms of intentionality as collective beliefs and collective desires. . . . Collective intentionality is the basis of all society, human or animal. . . . Indeed, I will define a social fact as any fact involving the collective intentionality of two or more agents." (Searle, 1995, p. 6)

administrative framework that juxtaposes individuals' existing ideas and skills in particular configurations (selective connections). The framework provides the context in which individuals develop new ideas and skills. (And an administrative framework is itself subject to change through the actions of its managers and their interpretation of the consequences.) In Penrose's view, the resources within a firm consist of the knowledge and skills of individuals (their capabilities) and the links between them (organizational capabilities). The firm frames the interactions that stimulate new connections within particular brains – and because these selective connections imply a choice, and all choices entail opportunity costs, it also impedes the development of ideas and skills that would be encouraged in other contexts. In Penrose's theory, as well as in Barnard's (1938), the development of new resources "in the course of current activities leads to the imagination of new productive services and thence to the imagination of new productive opportunities." (Loasby, 2008, p. 9) Penrose insists that "connections are made within a particular human mind [and thus a product of intentionality]; but the ordering of knowledge within this mind has been influenced, though not determined, by the context in which the order has emerged." (Loasby, 2008, p. 9)

Organizations are also tremendously efficient knowledge buffers, saving enormous amounts of cognitive resources that can be used for planning and experimentation. They import knowledge from outside and thus incorporate external knowledge depending on the knowledge they already possess. The ability to absorb knowledge and build structures of knowledge creates patterns in which certain kinds of external knowledge will fit according to criteria of similarity, because knowledge is constructed within domains. On many occasions, these patterns are typically incompatible with other kinds of external knowledge, which may seem nonsensical or even unnoticed. Institutions and organizations also provide the necessary stability to agents in planning. Without a minimum of stability in proceeding and organizing cooperation between agents, the problems associated with uncertainty would be insurmountable. However, stability also allows us to evaluate, as if it were the conditions of a laboratory, the consequences of experimenting with new courses of action (new conjectures). Stability is necessary for agents' adaptation and learning. "All orderly processes require institutions; these institutions need not – indeed should not – be static, but to be effective they must change more slowly than the processes which they support" (Loasby, 2018, p. 65). Of course, institutions are not exempt from the effects of bounded rationality and imperfect knowledge, and institutions and social rules in general are liable to have unintended consequences, which increase complexity, as Kelly observed.

Finally, institutions are focusing devices. Contrary to conventional models in economics, in which "individuals deal directly with the problems that they face, in all their complexity, and have no need for any structure to help them to cope" (Loasby, 2018, pp. 64–65), boundedly rational human beings (including economists) face an unknowable future. To deploy intelligent action, individuals need some limits (or constraints) to operate. Such limits are supplied by a host of institutions, which vary enormously in their prescriptiveness and power – they constrain behavior as the "rules of the game" in a football match, as North (1990, 2005) reminds us. Thus, a basic function of institutions is to channel the activities of actors with a constitutional lack of knowledge and to allow coordination. Appropriate and effective institutions within any organization and in any field of study lower the costs of transactions, but institutions cannot be created by individual choice. Institutions lower transaction costs because they do (to a greater or lesser extent) predict the behavior of other individuals and organizations we interact with. Institutions are ways of providing the capabilities that allow people to cope, in varying degrees, with an unknowable future. This enables individuals and organizations to plan and minimize the transaction costs associated with interaction.

4.5 Evolutionary Efficiency

Interaction also influences the efficiency of intentional action. As shown in Section 3.5, it is only possible to establish full judgment on the evolutionary efficiency of action at the micro (agent) level of interaction. However, as the deployment of individual action in society only makes sense in an interactive environment, the microlevel evolutionary efficiency criterion must be open to a dimension that goes beyond the individual. This characteristic requires that we evaluate the performance of a system at a higher level of interaction, where actions and their consequences are made explicit. Thus, the efficiency criterion addresses the *adequacy* of the connections and *alignments* between the agents' goals, intentions, and expectations as they interact within a particular socioeconomic system – an organization, firm, industry, economic sector, or the entire economy. Consequently, an evolutionary efficiency criterion must be consistent with one rooted at the micro level, but with effects observable at the meso level. Making abstraction of the institutional setting,[44] if we focus on the performance of a system at the meso level, performance is *high* when the alignment of the goals and actions of the agents "causes" the achievement of their pursued goals.

[44] Of course, different social arrangements will have different consequences in terms of coordination. For example, Harper (2013), revisiting Israel M. Kirzner's work, stresses the role of the system of property rights of a society to have a better understanding of the logic of economic coordination.

In other words, it can be said that the system is *evolutionary efficient*.[45] On the contrary, the performance of a system is *low* if the results are inadequate, meaning that deployed actions do not proceed as planned and do not lead to the achievement of the pursued objectives. This is the case of an *evolutionary inefficient* system: The system may allow the fulfillment of the objectives of some agents but block, limit, or ration other agents' goals. Examples of this are involuntary unemployment and underinvestment, as in Keynes (1936) and Malinvaud (1977), evolutionary traps, and so on. Internal inconsistencies in objectives and conflicting goals lead to rationing of goal satisfaction, resulting in a deterioration in the efficiency of agents' actions at the meso level.

If we consider the *social balance* resulting from the concurrence of all agents, represented by their individual dynamics, three extreme cases emerge. In the first one, all agents individually generate feasible action plans, so that, for each agent and their selected plan of action, the interactive deployment of actual actions effectively results in what was planned by each agent. This is the situation corresponding to a Walrasian General Equilibrium, where plans are a priori consistent and compatible: All agents (consumers and producers) effectively achieve the goals specified in their plans. In this case, there is efficiency at the meso level since all plans are simultaneously possible and all connections for all agents are *suitable*. In a second case, all agents form plans that, when individually considered, do not produce the desired effects: they are unfeasible. These plans are inefficient because the selected, interactively deployed action plans do not effectively produce what was planned and therefore do not effectively lead to the objectives included in the plans for any agent. In the third case, plans are individually consistent but unfeasible when interacting with other plans. Cases two and three generate rationed action: Effective future individual states differ and, in some cases, are "worse" or not as good as expected. In those circumstances, some agents may learn and then remove (at least partially) some of the sources of inefficiency (e.g., by forming new plans). In contrast, others may continue to commit the same errors.

This discussion on evolutionary efficiency resembles Hayek's (1937) analysis on the coordination of plans. For Hayek, the economic equilibrium is an equilibrium of expectations. However, our approach offers a broader consideration of the sources of inefficiency and reserves a special role for the intention to remove those inconsistencies or inefficiencies. A detailed explanation of how different scenarios could emerge is provided in Muñoz and Encinar (2019, pp. 932–933).

---

45 A limit case is the Walrasian General Equilibrium (Debreu, 1959), where all consumption and production plans are mutually compatible a priori. However, in true dynamic processes, the usual situation is the presence of goal conflicts. Muñoz and Encinar (2014b) provide some examples.

5 Evolution

5.1 Coordination and Reflexivity

A society, whatever imperfect it might be, is an order, and an order implies coordination. Hayek (1937, p. 41) raised the question of the coordination of planned action. For him, equilibrium means the compatibility of the different plans the individuals composing the society have made for action. In this sense, economic equilibrium may be understood as an equilibrium of expectations. (In a somewhat similar vein, Hahn (1974 [1984]) refers to equilibrium as a situation in which agents' policies, as he calls courses of action, do not change.) In Atemporal Walrasian general equilibrium theory, ex ante feasibility and consistency of plans are essential properties for coordination (see Debreu, 1959, p. 100). Exchange and production only take place at equilibrium prices, assuring full coordination. However, in (more realistic) historical processes, ex post coordination is by no means guaranteed due to interaction. On the contrary, the default state is out-of-equilibrium (Antonelli, 2011). This fact causes the continued evaluation and revision of plans and intentions. Revision provides a basic feedback mechanism that continuously renews the source of variety, including novelties, that feed evolutionary processes. Revision is at the base of learning. Soros (2013) refers to this feedback mechanism as reflexivity. Reflexivity can manifest in different ways, depending on the nature of the feedback mechanisms individuals use, and establishes a bidirectional connection between the formation of plans and the evaluation of outcomes in terms of achieving the pursued goals (see Figure 3). Like technologies, routines, and norms, successful courses of action are retained and replicated; the others are revised, removed, or abandoned in a replication-like process (Almudí & Fatás-Villafranca, 2018). Reflexivity establishes a dynamic nexus between individual and social reality. Of course, reflexivity does not necessarily imply increased coordination by itself; on the contrary, it is perfectly possible to have a type of revision of plans that involves even greater discoordination of individual and social processes, because reflexivity can introduce or reinforce biases in action.

5.2 From Micro to Meso, and from Meso to Macro

Traditionally, economics has distinguished between two levels of interaction: the micro level (that of individual agents and organizations) and the macro level (that of society or the economy as a whole). Initially, this distinction was introduced by Frisch (1933), who distinguished between microdynamics and macrodynamics. After Keynes' *General Theory*, which introduced the foundations of macroeconomic analysis as we know it today, Samuelson (1948) popularized the "didactic" division between micro- and macroeconomics. More recently, Dopfer and his coauthors have added a third level: the mesoeconomic level. The result is the micro–meso–macro framework, introduced in evolutionary economics by Dopfer et al. (2004) and developed more in depth by Dopfer and Potts (2008). The micro–meso–macro approach offers a comprehensive understanding of economic change as an evolutionary process. This framework diverges from classical and neoclassical economic models by emphasizing the role of innovation, knowledge diffusion, and the complexity of economic structures, and can be combined naturally with our approach, as we will see.

The micro–meso–macro framework is a hierarchical model used to explain how economic change occurs through the interactions and transformations of economic agents, structures, and systems.[46] It posits that economic evolution unfolds across the abovementioned three distinct but interconnected levels. First, the microlevel represents individual economic agents, such as firms, consumers, and entrepreneurs. It is the domain of individual actions and decisions, driven by the motivations, intentions, knowledge, and behaviors of micro agents. At the micro level, innovation often originates through the creation of new ideas, products, or processes. Second, the meso level acts as an intermediary between microlevel activities and macro-level outcomes. It is the level at which new knowledge or innovations become embedded as rules, routines, or practices that guide the behavior of economic agents. Meso structures represent the adoption and diffusion of these rules throughout the economy, facilitating the transition from individual innovation to widespread economic impact. And third, the macro level encompasses the entire economic system and represents aggregated outcomes of meso-level structures. It is where collective patterns, economic growth, and structural shifts become visible. The accumulation and interaction of meso-level elements cause changes at the macro level.

Economic evolution begins at the micro level by introducing a new combination, likely a Schumpeterian novelty, and typically a new combination of actions (means) and goals (ends) within a plan. Microlevel activity involves experimentation, creativity, and the intentional pursuit of opportunities. Microlevel agents are influenced by their environment (mainly social) and existing meso-level structures, which shape their behaviors and decision-making processes. However, agents can also disrupt these structures by introducing innovations that challenge established norms.

The meso level is the core of evolutionary processes. It captures the life-cycle of rules – from origination and adoption to eventual obsolescence or

[46] The following argument in this section follows Earl and Muñoz (2027b).

integration into broader macro structures. Meso rules are codified knowledge or practices that are replicated across the economy. Dopfer et al. (2004) describe meso units as the carriers of economic knowledge, acting as templates for action that guide microlevel agents. The meso level is dynamic: new rules compete with existing ones, leading to a selection process where only the most adaptive or beneficial combinations of rules, skills, capabilities, technologies, plans ... survive and spread. Diffusion leads to shifts in the economic landscape as new meso-rules replace outdated ones or coexist with established practices, fostering diversity and complexity within the economic system.

Ultimately, the accumulation of meso-level changes culminates in macro-level transformations. The macro level reflects the emergent properties of the entire economic system, encompassing growth patterns, structural changes, and economic cycles. Dopfer and Potts (2008) argue that macroeconomic phenomena cannot be fully understood without considering the underlying meso processes. For instance, economic growth is viewed as a macro-level outcome of continuous meso-level innovations that permeate the economy and transform it over time. This view challenges traditional macroeconomic models that treat the economy as a system in equilibrium, suggesting instead that economic systems are inherently dynamic and subject to constant evolutionary pressures.

In terms of plans of action, the framework outlines several mechanisms that drive the micro–meso–macro transition. At the microlevel, the process begins with creating a new plan. Next comes the adoption and diffusion phase. This phase occurs at the meso level, where new plans (and new combinations in general) are adopted by other agents and integrated into their routines or practices. Successful plans spread throughout the economy, influencing the behavior of micro agents and becoming an integral part of the economic structure. Courses of action that prove beneficial (efficient) are retained and embedded in the meso layer, contributing to the stability of the macro system. Inefficient or outdated courses of action at the base of meso structures may become obsolete as innovations arise, leading to continuous economic evolution.

Dopfer and Potts (2008) also discuss the concept of meso trajectories, which are pathways that meso rules follow from their inception to full integration into the macro system. These trajectories are not linear; they involve periods of rapid change, stability, and decline, reflecting the cyclical nature of economic evolution. This perspective provides an alternative explanation for economic cycles, which traditional models often attribute to external shocks or policy changes. Instead, evolutionary economics views these cycles as the result of the internal dynamics of meso-level interactions and the diffusion of innovations.[47]

The micro–meso–macro framework provides a powerful lens for understanding the role of intentionality in economic evolution. The framework highlights the importance of meso-level structures as the central component through which microlevel innovations are translated into macro-level outcomes. This perspective acknowledges the complex, adaptive, and nonlinear nature of economic systems, offering new insights into the mechanisms of growth, innovation, and structural change. However, although it underscores that economic evolution is not just a matter of individual actions or aggregate outcomes but also the dynamic interplay of rules and routines that shape and reshape the economy over time, it recognizes the critical role of the internal dimension of action in that anything in the system relies at the end of the day in what agents have in their minds (remember Figure 1).

5.3 The Economy as an Ecology of Plans

Richard E. Wagner has proposed a shift in perspective to enhance macroeconomic analysis. In his view, the macroeconomy is the outcome of an ecology of plans (Wagner, 2012). A change in economic architecture (markets, sectors, etc.) is the result of people acting intentionally to alleviate uneasiness. Wagner reimagines the macroeconomy not as a simple aggregation of microlevel decisions but as a complex, dynamic network where individual actions and plans interact to create emergent properties at the macro level. As Schelling (1978) and others previously noted,[48] Wagner's approach highlights that macroeconomic phenomena are inherently more complex than the sum of individual microlevel actions due to the unpredictable interactions between plans. Unlike traditional macroeconomic models that treat the macroeconomy as a scaled-up version of microlevel behavior (e.g., representative agent models), Wagner's framework views macro-level outcomes as emergent properties. These emergent structures and their properties are not predictable by simply analyzing individual actions because they depend on the interactions among numerous

[47] The implications of this analytical framework for economic theory and policy are straightforward. Policy interventions should consider the interplay between microlevel agents, meso-level structures, and macro-level outcomes. This approach shifts focus from aggregate demand management to structural and institutional support for evolutionary ecosystems. Additionally, economic development is path-dependent, shaped by past meso rules that influence current and future economic trajectories. Understanding these features should help policymakers create conditions that allow for flexibility and adaptation of actual economic processes that unfold over time.

[48] Schelling's (1978) exemplifies how simple, intentional decisions by individuals can collectively lead to complex societal outcomes.

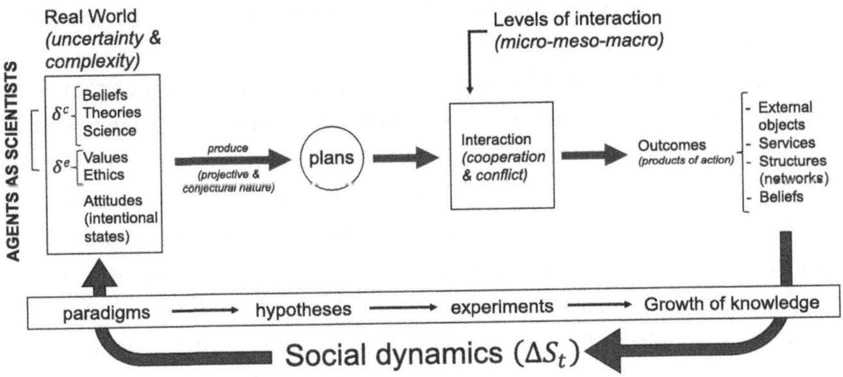

Figure 5 Individual basis and social dynamics.

plans. As in Hayek, under this interpretation, economic and social processes are out-of-equilibrium processes. This ecological approach rejects the equilibrium-centric view (that dominates mainstream economics) and accepts that economies operate in a state of constant change and nonequilibrium. Consequently, macroeconomic order is incomplete and constantly evolving, driven by the continuous introduction, revision, and abandonment of plans by agents within the economy. Interactions between individual plans result in spontaneous order, an order that arises organically from the decentralized activities of individuals and organizations, rather than being imposed from above. Turbulence and change are inherent to this ecology, driven by the fact that no agent can fully anticipate all the implications of their plans due to the limited and dispersed nature of their knowledge.

Figure 5 represents the passage between the individual level (microlevel) in which plans are formed internally (in the prefrontal cortex of the brain using mental models, local knowledge, and accumulated experience) as a result of the cognitive and ethical dynamics of the agents, and the cultural context (which includes institutions) in which the agents have been immersed, and the external, meso and macro planes. The interaction of intentional action (embodied in action plans) within the system generates the products of action (objects, services, structures, beliefs, and knowledge . . .). These products are compared with previous states and with the conditions of satisfaction of the agents' beliefs and desires. In this way, the conjectures and expectations of the agents (again incorporated into their plans) are experimented with and tested against the historical reality being produced. The mismatches between what is intentionally sought and what is obtained trigger the processes of review and reformulation of plans. Miscoordination is a natural phenomenon in an ecology of plans, as individual plans seldom align perfectly. This framework explains why economies experience fluctuations and why perfect coordination, assumed in equilibrium models, rarely exists.

A central theoretical implication of the economy as an ecology of plans is the emphasis on understanding over prediction. Since emergent phenomena are inherently complex and adaptive, policy implications must be flexible and context-specific. The economy as an ecology of plans framework acknowledges that knowledge within an economy is dispersed (a typical Austrian assumption) and that interactions between diverse plans generate turbulence as a normal condition. This turbulence should be seen as a system feature, not an anomaly. Consequently, policy interventions are part of the network of interactions rather than external levers.[49] Like other agents, policymakers operate within the ecology and contribute to the macro-level outcomes through their intentions, goals, actions, and interactions.

To sum up, the ecology of plans perspective redefines macroeconomics as the study of how complex systems of individual actions and plans give rise to emergent macro-level phenomena. This approach highlights that macro-level coordination, order, and turbulence are natural products of microlevel planning and interaction, challenging policymakers and economists to appreciate the limits of control and the importance of adaptability within economic systems.

5.4 The Economy as a Complex Evolutionary Process

Economies are complex evolving systems. For the economy to be a complex system, some important features are needed: agents must be heterogeneous and have partial or imperfect knowledge about other agents; they inhabit a world of uncertainty and complexity; they must, therefore, try to make sense of the situation they face using cognitive patterns and imagination; they also pursue different and usually conflicting goals; there is "no global controller" and the workings of these systems is not the result of the intentions or action plans of a centralized authority or planner; interaction is dispersed and local, and agents may (or may not) adapt to continually changing circumstances and the emergence of perpetual novelty. The outcome is a complex evolving system that displays out-of-equilibrium dynamics, patterns, and emergent phenomena not visible to equilibrium analysis.

What is the role of action plans and intentionality in this context? Arthur's *Complexity Economics* (Arthur, 2015) highlights that intentional actions taken

[49] Unlike models where disturbances are attributed to external shocks, Wagner's approach treats them as internal features of the interactions between diverse, evolving plans. He uses examples: unemployment resulting from wage premiums, monetary policy, and central banking. Agents' actions influence the system indirectly through networks of interactions with other microlevel entities, making the results of policy interventions emergent rather than direct.

by agents, influenced by their expectations and adaptive strategies, are key to understanding nonlinear economic outcomes. Arthur's contributions, particularly his emphasis on increasing returns and network effects, reinforce the idea that economic systems evolve through interactions that create path-dependent and emergent outcomes. This perspective, which combines complexity with evolution, views the economy not as a static entity seeking equilibrium, but as a dynamic, adaptive system characterized by innovation, adaptation, and continuous transformation. Economies are not static entities but living systems that continuously evolve through innovation, competition, and adaptation. Economic agents (firms, consumers, and institutions) do not operate under perfect information or rational optimization but adapt based on learning, experimentation, and environmental feedback.[50] Economies operate far from equilibrium. This circumstance is not a defect of economic systems; on the contrary, it enables economies to be dynamic, adaptive, and subject to constant change. Thus, economic systems evolve and transform qualitatively over time through mechanisms similar to those found in biological evolution. Arthur presents the economy as a complex adaptive system influenced by cumulative innovations, path dependency, and increasing returns.[51]

Unlike neoclassical economics, which often treats economic change as exogenous, evolutionary economics places innovation (recombinations) at the core of economic processes. Innovations emerge at the micro level through the actions of individuals and firms, gradually diffusing throughout the economy and influencing the behavior of other agents, ultimately leading to structural changes. This process results in an economy characterized by ongoing flux and nonequilibrium dynamics, where stability is temporary and periods of turbulence and adjustment are the norm. Once innovations appear, economic evolution is driven by a selection mechanism in which successful innovations and strategies are adopted and replicated, while less effective ones are discarded. This mirrors the natural selection process in biological evolution, where traits that confer an advantage are more likely to persist. Firms and institutions adapt to changes in their environment by experimenting with new strategies, resulting in a constantly evolving economic landscape. Retention implies changes in knowledge bases, adjustments of skills, routines, and capabilities, as well as norms and institutions. These changes may give rise to path dependence phenomena. Initial conditions and early choices can have long-term

[50] This perspective aligns with Schumpeter's concept of *creative destruction*. See Schumpeter (1943 [1996]) and Antonelli and Colombelli (2025).

[51] The core principles of evolutionary economics are dynamism and change, new combinations as the driving force of evolution, selection and adaptation algorithms (Beinhocker, 2011), path dependence, and historical contingency.

impacts due to increasing returns, lock-in effects, and positive feedback loops. Once an economic pathway is established, it becomes self-reinforcing, making it difficult for alternative paths to emerge. This explains why certain technologies or industries dominate even when superior alternatives exist, highlighting the role of cumulative causation in economic systems. Interconnected agents in the system are adaptive; they learn from their experiences and adjust their behavior, contributing to an economy that is always in a state of becoming, rather than being.

One of Arthur's seminal contributions is his theory of *increasing returns*, which challenges the traditional assumption of diminishing returns prevalent in classical economics. Increasing returns occur when the benefits of adopting a particular technology or strategy increase as more people adopt it. This concept helps explain the dominance of specific technologies and firms in the market, as early advantages can lead to a self-reinforcing process where the winners continue to gain market share.[52] Arthur's work also highlights how positive feedback loops in economic systems can lead to path dependence. A reinforcing cycle ensues when a particular choice becomes increasingly advantageous as more agents opt for it. This can result in market outcomes contingent on historical events rather than inherent efficiencies. These feedback loops explain why economies can become locked into suboptimal paths and why changing established norms or technologies can be challenging. Finally, another critical aspect of Arthur's analysis is the concept of network effects (Kirman, 1997), where the value of a product or service increases as more people use it – a phenomenon that is particularly relevant in the digital economy. Network effects contribute to increasing returns and the persistence of specific economic structures, reinforcing that economic processes are evolutionary and path-dependent.

When combined with broader evolutionary economics, Arthur's complexity framework portrays the economy as a system that evolves through the interaction of heterogeneous agents. These agents are not perfectly rational but boundedly rational, operating under limited information and uncertainty. Within the ontological constraints of the world they inhabit, agents learn, adapt, and coevolve, thereby creating a constantly changing economic environment. This behavior ensures that the economy remains in a state of perpetual motion, adapting to new conditions and reshaping itself. The economy can no longer be seen as a collection of objects, but as a network of intentional actions; it is not an economy of nouns, but an economy of verbs (Arthur, 2023).

---

[52] Arthur used the case of the QWERTY keyboard (David, 1985) to demonstrate how increasing returns can lock in a particular technology even if it is not the most efficient option.

6 Conclusion

To deal with uncertainty and complexity, economic agents, using their imagination, "invent" conjectures about future states of the system and continuously form new plans because the outcomes they must respond to are novel. The result is a complex, evolving system that is inherently unpredictable and continually reconstructing. Strategies evolve, time assumes significance, structures take shape, and new structures and phenomena emerge. Economic agents continually adjust their actions and strategies in response to the outcomes resulting from their interactions. This iterative process modifies the socioeconomic system, necessitating further adaptation. Consequently, agents live in an "ecosystem" where their beliefs, values, and intentions form intentional courses of action and strategies that are continuously tested for survival within an "ecology" that is simultaneously shaped and disrupted by their behavior. Complexity economics seeks to understand how actions, strategies, or expectations can evolve in response to the patterns they contribute to forming. (Gallegati & Gallegati, 2025, pp. 3069–3073)

The arguments presented in this Element to explain evolution and complexity are consistent with the categories of intentionality – beliefs, desires, expectations, intention, collective intentionality – their role in cognitive sciences and social philosophy, and the explanation of individual and collective behavior. Our central claim is that intentionality is a key constituent of human action and is at the origin of emergent properties within socioeconomic complex evolving systems. "It is the inherent dynamic dimension of intentions and goals that makes the individual and organizational capabilities truly evolutionary . . . The cognitive, ethical, and cultural dynamics (within which the categories of intention operate) that govern the processes of formation, selection, and deployment of plans are then at the base of the meso" (Muñoz et al., 2011, p. 200).[53] The structure of agents' intentionality is what generates the dynamics, from which results, among other things, social structures. Intentions incorporate what is known, desired, judged good or bad, from a cultural point of view. Changes in agents' intentionality – linked to the conception of new goals – renew agents' action plans and reshape social interactions.

Intentionality also binds the actions and goals of individuals and organizations, providing them with meaning. This is particularly clear when we use the analytical template that provides the action plan approach. To be meaningful, there must always be a direction of action; otherwise, action is directed by the ultimate goals pursued by agents. In this sense, intentionality, which poses and hierarchically organizes agents' goals, provides meaning to actions deployed by

[53] On the influence of cultural dynamics on evolutionary processes, see Witt (2008).

individuals and organizations. As we have shown, all intentional elements can be analytically integrated into action plans, the basic structure of our evolutionary analytical framework, which is particularly useful for understanding decision processes, human (economic and social) action, and the emergence of complexity. The action plan approach also enables us to accommodate intentionality into economics when we understand the economy as an "ecology of plans" (Wagner, 2012, 2020). Thus, an economy's "macro state" results from the interaction of action plans loaded with agents' intentionality. The macro state and its evolution are something agents are producing and, for this reason, are not a mere "external" or "objective" reality, but the practical reality that agents are producing from their subjectivity. In an evolutionary interpretation, efficiency is achieved when the outcomes of deployed actions align with the reality produced by the interaction of those actions. This approach's main topics are emergent properties, error, and learning.

Many other factors explain the evolution of complex socioeconomic systems. Agents are intrinsically heterogeneous, differing in endowments, skills, capabilities, size, location, and other characteristics. They also vary in their knowledge, beliefs, and visions of the world. There are different cultural systems and technological regimes at work, as well as shocks external to socioeconomic systems – such as earthquakes and pandemics. And all kinds of endogenously generated novelties (technical, ethical, and cultural). Even so, intentionality remains a key factor in understanding the dynamics of human complex, evolving, adaptive systems. However, intentionality has been blurred (or is absent) in economics. In most literature and formal models, agents are portrayed as automata that react to changes in the environment (such as prices, market structures, and technology) and are unable to pursue their interests intentionally (Rosser, 2004). In such cases, the primary source of novelties usually remains obscure and basically unexplained.[54] Of course, the enormous advances made in evolutionary economics, the important contributions of Austrian economics (especially Hayek), recent developments in institutional and behavioral economics (Earl, 2022), experimental economics, neuroeconomics, cognitive economics (Viale, 2027), and complexity studies must be recognized. However, in general, there is an analytical gap that unifies all these approaches to complex evolving economic processes, a gap that could be filled by evolutionary economists.

The analytical consideration of intentionality has important practical uses. Some examples include the study of entrepreneurship, the relationship between

[54] A circumstance that occurs even, paradoxically, in the case of Schumpeter, as Encinar and Muñoz (2006) have shown.

psychology and economics, innovation, the role of ethics, and the consequences of social and cultural trends, among others. Understanding the role of intentionality in economic evolution has policy implications. Policymakers, viewed as agents with their intentions, contribute to shaping economic outcomes through regulations, incentives, and strategic initiatives. However, the evolutionary nature of the economy implies that policies should be adaptive and responsive to the evolving behavior of economic agents. For example, in the case of analyzing innovation systems and economic evolution, policy should not only react to existing conditions but also anticipate and facilitate the intentional behavior of agents that drives innovation and structural change.

In this Element, we have attempted to demonstrate that intentionality is always at the root of emergent orders that result from human interaction. Orders that are of an increasing degree of complexity. Economics should pay more attention to understanding what agents try to do (and why), what makes it possible to at least partially understand the drift of evolution, and, eventually, the rational possibility of influencing reality, as far as possible. A new combination of methodologies and multidisciplinary approaches would be needed. If our argument is correct, special attention should be paid to the formation and alignment of the intentions (expressed as goals) of the agents involved in complex socioeconomic systems at all their levels (micro, meso, and macro). This is a very promising research project, and this Element tries to be a modest contribution to advancing in that direction.

References

Almudí, I., & Fatás-Villafranca, F. (2018). Promotion and Coevolutionary Dynamics in Contemporary Capitalism. *Journal of Economic Issues, LII* (1), 80–102. https://doi.org/10.1080/00213624.2018.1430943.

Almudi, I., Fatas-Villafranca, F., & Sanchez-Choliz, J. (2016). A Formal Discussion of the Sarewitz-Nelson Rules. *Economics of Innovation and New Technology*, *25*(7), 714–730. http://dx.doi.org/10.1080/10438599.2015.1133042.

Anscombe, G. E. M. (1957). *Intention*. Oxford: Blackwell.

Antonelli, C. (2011). The Economic Complexity of Technological Change: Knowledge Interaction and Path Dependence. In C. Antonelli (Ed.), *Handbook on the Economic Complexity of Technological Change* (pp. 3–59). Cheltenham: Edward Elgar.

Antonelli, C., & Colombelli, A. (2025). The Creative Response: The Schumpeterian Legacy. *Eurasian Business Review*. https://doi.org/10.1007/s40821-025-00298-7.

Arthur, W. B. (2015). *Complexity and the Economy*. New York: Oxford University Press.

Arthur, W. B. (2023). Economics in Nouns and Verbs. *Journal of Economic Behavior & Organization*, *205*, 638–647. https://doi.org/10.1016/j.jebo.2022.10.036.

Axtell, R. L., & Farmer, J. D. (2025). Agent-Based Modeling in Economics and Finance: Past, Present, and Future. *Journal of Economic Literature*, *63*(1), 197–287. https:doi.org/10.1257/jel.20221319.

Barnard, C. (1938). *The Functions of the Executive*. Cambridge, MA: Harvard University Press.

Baumol, W. J. (1990). Entrepreneurship: Productive, Unproductive, and Destructive. *Journal of Political Economy*, *98*(3), 893–921.

Becker, M. C. (2004). Organizational Routines: A Review of the Literature. *Industrial and Corporate Change*, *13*(4), 643–678.

Beinhocker, E. D. (2006). *The Origin of Wealth: Evolution, Complexity and the Radical Remaking of Economics*. Boston, MA: Harvard Business School Press.

Beinhocker, E. D. (2011). Evolution as Computation: Integrating Self-organization with Generalized Darwinism. *Journal of Institutional Economics*, *7*(3), 393–423. https://doi.org/10.1017/S1744137411000257.

Beinhocker, E. D. (2013). Reflexivity, Complexity, and the Nature of Social Science. *Journal of Economic Methodology, 20*(4), 330–342. https://doi.org/10.1080/1350178X.2013.859403.

Bianchi, M. (Ed.) (1998). *The Active Consumer. Novelty and Surprise in Consumer Choice*. London: Routledge.

Blind, G. D. (2017). *The Entrepreneur in Rule-Based Economics. Theory, Empirical Practice, and Policy Design*. Cham: Springer International Publishing AG.

Boulding, K.E. (1981). Evolutionary Economics. Beverly Hills: Sage.

Boulding, K. E. (1991). What is Evolutionary Economics? *Journal of Evolutionary Economics*, *1*(1), 9–17.

Bratman, M. E. (1999 [1987]). *Intention, Plans, and Practical Reason*. Stanford: CSLI.

Bratman, M. E. (2007). *Structures of Agency*. New York: Oxford University Press.

Brentano, F. (1874 [1995]). *Psychology from an Empirical Standpoint*. London: Routledge.

Cañibano, C., Encinar, M. I., & Muñoz, F.-F. (2006). "*Ethical Novelty*": *New Insights into Economic Change*. Retrieved from Madrid: http://econpapers.repec.org/RePEc:uam:wpaper:200603.

Cañibano, C., Encinar, M. I., & Muñoz, F.-F. (2017). The Economic Rationality of Novative Behaviour. In B. Godin & D. Vinck (Eds.), *Critical Studies of Innovation. Alternative Approaches to the Pro-innovation Bias* (pp. 240–256). Cheltenham: Edward Elgar.

Casson, M. (1982). *The Entrepreneur: An Economic Theory*. Totowa, NJ: Barnes and Noble Books.

Crespo, R. F. (2013). Two Conceptions of Economics and Maximisation. *Cambridge Journal of Economics*, *37*(4), 759–774. https://doi.org/10.1093/cje/bes076.

Damasio, A. (1994). *Descartes' Error: Emotion, Reason, and the Human Brain*. New York: Putnam.

David, P. A. (1985). Clio and the Economics of QWERTY. *The American Economic Review*, *75*(2), 332–337.

Debreu, G. (1959). *Theory of Value. An Axiomatic Analysis of Economic Equilibrium*. New Heaven: Yale University Press.

Dekker, E., & Remic, B. (2027). The Epistemic Function of Institutions. In R. Viale (Ed.), *Elgar Handbook of Cognitive Economics*. Cheltenham: Edward Elgar.

Denzau, A. T., & North, D. C. (1994). Shared Mental Models: Ideologies and Institutions. *Kyklos*, *47*(1), 3–31.

Dopfer, K. (2005). Evolutionary Economics: A Theoretical Framework. In K. Dopfer (Ed.), *The Evolutionary Foundations of Economics* (pp. 3–55). Cambridge: Cambridge University Press.

Dopfer, K. (2011). Mesoeconomics: A Unified Approach to System Complexity and Evolution. In C. Antonelli (Ed.), *Handbook on the Economic Complexity of Technological Change* (pp. 341–356). Cheltenham: Edward Elgar.

Dopfer, K., Foster, J., & Potts, J. (2004). Micro-meso-macro. *Journal of Evolutionary Economics*, *14*(3), 263–279. https://doi.org/10.1007/s00191-004-0193-0.

Dopfer, K., & Potts, J. (2008). *The General Theory of Economic Evolution*. New York: Routledge.

Dopfer, K., & Potts, J. (2009). On the Theory of Economic Evolution. *Evolutionary and Institutional Economics Review*, *6*(1), 23–44.

Dopfer, K., Potts, J., & Pyka, A. (2016). Upward and Downward Complementarity: The Meso Core of Evolutionary Growth Theory. *Journal of Evolutionary Economics*, *26*(4), 1–11. https://doi.org/10.1007/s00191-015-0434-4.

Dosi, G., & Nelson, R. R. (1994). An Introduction to Evolutionary Theories in Economics. *Journal of Evolutionary Economics*, *4*(3), 153–172. https://doi.org/10.1007/BF01236366.

Earl, P. E. (1983). *The Economic Imagination: Towards a Behavioural Analysis of Choice*. Brighton: Wheatsheaf Books.

Earl, P. E. (1992). The Complementarity of Economic Applications of Cognitive Dissonance Theory and Personal Construct Psychology. In S. E. G. Lea, P. Webley, and B. Young (Eds.) *New Directions in Economic Psychology* (pp. 49–65). Aldershot: Edward Elgar.

Earl, P. E. (2003). The Entrepreneur as a Constructor of Connections. In R. Koppl (Ed.), *Austrian Economics and Entrepreneurial Studies*. Oxford: JAI-Elsevier Science, 113–130.

Earl, P. E. (2022). *Principles of Behavioral Economics. Bringing Together Old, New and Evolutionary Approaches*. Cambridge: Cambridge University Press.

Earl, P. E., & Muñoz, F.-F. (2027a). The Growth of Knowledge Approach to Economics: Brian J. Loasby and the Stirling School. In R. Viale (Ed.), *The Elgar Handbook of Cognitive Economics*. Cheltenham: Edward Elgar.

Earl, P. E., & Muñoz, F.-F. (2027b). Cognition and the Uptake of Innovations: A Micro–Meso-Macro Perspective. In R. Viale (Ed.), *The Elgar Handbook of Cognitive Economics*. Cheltenham: Edward Elgar.

Earl, P. E., & Potts, J. (2004). Bounded Rationality and Decomposability: The Basis for Integrating Cognitive and Evolutionary Economics. In M. Augier & J. G. March (Eds.), *Models of a Man: Essays in Memory of Herbert A. Simon* (pp. 317–333). Cambridge, MA: The MIT Press.

Encinar, M. I. (2002). *Análisis de las propiedades de "consistencia" y "realizabilidad" en los planes de acción. Una perspectiva desde la teoría Económica*. Universidad Autónoma de Madrid, Madrid.

Encinar, M. I., & Muñoz, F.-F. (2006). On Novelty and Economics: Schumpeter's Paradox. *Journal of Evolutionary Economics*, *16*(3), 255–277. https://doi.org/10.1007/s00191-006-0018-4.

Eucken, W. (1940). *Die Grunlagen der Nationalökonomie*. Jena: Gustav Fischer.

Felin, T., & Foss, N. J. (2009). Organizational Routines and Capabilities: Historical Drift and a Course-Correction toward Microfoundations. *Scandinavian Journal of Management*, *25*, 157–167.

Frisch, R. (1933). Propagation Problems and Impulse Problems in Dynamic Economics. In *Economic Essays in Honour of Gustav Cassel* (pp. 171–205). London: George Allen & Unwin.

Frolov, D. (2024). The Economics of Cognitive Institutions: Mapping Debates, Looking Ahead. *Journal of Institutional Economics*, 20, e28, 1–20.

Fuster, J. M. (2003). *Cortex and Mind: Unifying Cognition*. New York: Oxford University Press.

Fuster, J. M. (2008). *The Prefrontal Cortex* (4th ed.). Amsterdam: Academic Press.

Fuster, J. M. (2011). Hayek in Today's Cognitive Neuroscience. In *Hayek in Mind: Hayek's Philosophical Psychology* (pp. 3–11).

Gallegati, M., & Gallegati, S. (2025). Why Does Economics Need Complexity? *Soft Computing*, *29*(6), 3063–3072. https://doi.org/10.1007/s00500-025-10548-5.

Ghoshal, S. (2005). Bad Management Theories Are Destroying Good Management Practices. *Academy of Management Learning & Education*, *4* (1), 75–91.

Gigerenzer, G. (2008). *Rationality for Mortals: How People Cope with Uncertainty*. Oxford: Oxford University Press.

Gigerenzer, G. (2021). Axiomatic Rationality and Ecological Rationality. *Synthese*, *198*(4), 3547–3564. https://doi.org/10.1007/s11229-019-02296-5.

Gigerenzer, G., & Selten, R. (Eds.). (2001). *Bounded Rationality: The Adaptive Toolbox*. Cambridge, MA: The MIT Press.

Godin, B. (2008). *Innovation: The History of a Category*. Retrieved from Montreal: www.csiic.ca/.

Hahn, F. H. (1974 [1984]). On the Notion of Equilibrium in Economics. In F. H. Hahn (Ed.), *Equilibrium and Macroeconomics* (pp. 43–71). Oxford: Basil Blackwell.

Harper, D. A. (1996). *Entrepreneurship and the Market Process*. London: Routledge.

Harper, D. A. (2003). Foundations of entrepreneurship and economic development. London & New York: Routledge.

Harper, D. A. (2013). Property Rights, Entrepreneurship and Coordination. *Journal of Economic Behavior & Organization*, *88*, 62–77. https://doi.org/10.1016/j.jebo.2011.10.018.

Harper, D. A., & Endres, A. M. (2012). The Anatomy of Emergence, with a Focus upon Capital Formation. *Journal of Economic Behavior & Organization*, 82(2–3), 352–367. https://doi.org/10.1016/j.jebo.2011.03.013.

Harper, D. A., Muñoz, F.-F., & Vázquez, F. J. (2021). Innovation in Online Higher-Education Services: Building Complex Systems. *Economics of Innovation and New Technology*, *30*(4), 412–431. https://doi.org/10.1080/10438599.2020.1716508.

Hayek, F. A. (1937). Economics and Knowledge. *Economica*, *4*(13), 33–54. https://doi.org/10.2307/2548786.

Hayek, F. A. (1945). The Use of Knowledge in Society. *American Economic Review*, *35*, 519–530.

Hayek, F. A. (1952). *The Sensory Order: An Inquiry into the Foundations of Theoretical Psychology*. Chicago: The University of Chicago Press.

Hicks, J. R. (1939). *Value and Capital: An Inquiry into Some Fundamental Principles of Economic Theory*. Oxford: Clarendon Paperbacks.

Hodgson, G. M., & Knudsen, T. (2006). Dismantling Lamarckism: Why Descriptions of Socio-Economic Evolution as Lamarckian are Misleading. *Journal of Evolutionary Economics*, *16*(4), 343–366.

Hodgson, G. M. (2006). What are institutions? *Journal of Economic Issues*, XL (1), 1–25.

Huerta de Soto, J. (2009). *The Theory of Dynamic Efficiency*. New York: Routledge.

Kahneman, D., & Tversky, A. (1979). Prospect Theory: An Analysis of Decision under Risk. *Econometrica*, *47*(2), 263–291.

Kauffman, S. A. (1993). *The Origins of Order: Self-organization and Selection in Evolution*. Oxford: Oxford University Press.

Kelly, G. A. (1955 [1963]). *A Theory of Personality*. New York: W.W. Norton.

Keynes, J. M. (1936). *The General Theory of Employment, Interest and Money*. London: MacMillan.

Kirman, A. (1997). The Economy as an Evolving Network. *Journal of Evolutionary Economics*, *7*, 339–353.

Kirzner, I. M. (1992). *The Meaning of the Market Process*. London: Routledge.

Knight, F. (1921). *Risk, Uncertainty and Profit*. Boston: Houghton Mifflin.

Koppl, R. (2002). Expectations. In *Big Players and the Economic Theory of Expectations* (pp. 96–119). London: Palgrave Macmillan.

Koppl, R., Kauffman, S., Felin, T., & Longo, G. (2015). Economics for a creative world. *Journal of Institutional Economics*, 11(1), 1–31.

Koppl, R., Devereaux, A., Herriot, J., & Kauffman, S. (2019). A Simple Combinatorial Model of World Economic History. arXiv:1811.04502v1.

Lachmann, L. M. (1951). The Science of Human Action. *Economica*, *18*(72), 412–427. https://doi.org/10.2307/2549611.

Lachmann, L. M. (1977). *Capital, Expectations, and the Market Process: Essays on the Theory of the Market Economy* (W. E. Grinder Ed.). Kansas City: Sheed Andrews and McMeel.

Lewis, P. A. (2017). Shackle on choice, imagination and creativity: Hayekian foundations. *Cambridge Journal of Economics*, 41(1), 1–24.

Loasby, B. J. (1971). Hypothesis and Paradigm in the Theory of the Firm. *The Economic Journal*, *81*(324), 863–885. https://doi.org.10.2307/2230322.

Loasby, B. J. (1976). *Choice, Complexity and Ignorance: An Enquiry into Economic Theory and the Practice of Decision Making*. Cambridge: Cambridge University Press.

Loasby, B. J. (1983). Knowledge, Learning and Enterprise. In J. Wiseman (Ed.), *Beyond Positive Economics? Proceedings of Section F (Economics) of the British Association for the Advancement of Science, York 1981* (pp. 104–121). London: Palgrave Macmillan.

Loasby, B. J. (1984). On Scientific Method. *Journal of Post Keynesian Economics*, 6(3), 394–410.

Loasby, B. J. (1989). *The Mind and Method of the Economist: A Critical Appraisal of Major Economists in the Twentieth Century*. Aldershot: Edward Elgar.

Loasby, B. J. (1998). The Concept of Capabilities. In N. J. Foss (Ed.), *Economic Organization, Capabilities and Coordination: Essays in Honour of G.B. Richardson* (pp. 163–182). London: Routledge.

Loasby, B. J. (1999). *Knowledge, Institutions and Evolution in Economics*. London: Routledge.

Loasby, B. J. (2000). How Do We Know? In P. E. Earl & S. F. Frowen (Eds.), *Economics as an Art of Thought. Essays in Memory of G.L.S. Shackle* (pp. 1–20). New York: Routledge.

Loasby, B. J. (2001). Time, Knowledge and Evolutionary Dynamics: Why Connections Matter. *Journal of Evolutionary Economics*, *11*(4), 393–412. https://doi.org/10.1007/PL00003867.

Loasby, B. J. (2003). Closed models and open systems. *Journal of Economic Methodology*, 10(3), 285-306.

Loasby, B. J. (2007). Entrepreneurship, Evolution and the Human Mind. In U. Cantner & F. Malerba (Eds.), *Innovation, Industrial Dynamics and Structural Transformation: Schumpeterian Legacies* (pp. 29–47). Heidelberg: Springer.

Loasby, B. J. (2008). La microfundamentación de las capacidades organizativas. In C. Cañibano, M. I. Encinar, & F. F. Muñoz (Eds.), *Economía del conocimiento y la innovación. Nuevas aproximaciones a una relación compleja* (pp. 35–58). Madrid: Ediciones Pirámide.

Loasby, B. J. (2009). Knowledge, Coordination and the Firm: Historical Perspectives. *The European Journal of the History of Economic Thought*, *16*(4), 539–558. https://doi.org/10.1080/09672560903201227.

Loasby, B. J. (2018). Missed Connections and Opportunities Forgone: A Counterfactual History of Twentieth-Century Economics. In A. Chai & U. Witt (Eds.), *Understanding Economic Change: Advances in Evolutionary Economics* (pp. 43–80). Cambridge: Cambridge University Press.

Malinvaud, E. (1977). *The Theory of Unemployment Reconsidered*. Basil: Blackwell.

Malinvaud, E. (1999). *Leçons de théorie microéconomique* (4e édition ed.). Paris: Dunod.

Marshall, A. (1868 [1994]). Ye Machine. In "*Alfred Marshall's Early Philosophical Writings*": *Research in the History of Economic Thought and Methodology, Archival Supplement 4*, 116–132.

Menger, C. (1871). *Grundsätze der Volkswirthschaftslehre*. Wien: Wilhelm Braumüller.

Metcalfe, J. S. (2004). The Entrepreneur and the Style of Modern Economics. *Journal of Evolutionary Economics*, *14*(2), 157–175. https://doi.org/10.1007/s00191-004-0210-3.

Miller, G. A., Galanter, E., & Pribram, K. H. (1960). *Plans and the Structure of Behavior*. New York: Holt, Rinehart and Winston.

Miller, J. H., & Page, S. E. (2007). *Complex Adaptive Systems: An Introduction to Computational Models of Social Life*. Princeton: Princeton University Press.

Mises, L. (1949). *Human Action: A Treatise on Economics*. New Haven: Yale University Press.

Muñoz, F.-F. (2024). The Coevolution of Technology, Markets, and Culture: The Challenging Case of AI. *Review of Evolutionary Political Economy*, 5(3), 511–533. https://doi.org/10.1007/s43253-024-00126-0.

Muñoz, F.-F., & Encinar, M. I. (2014a). Intentionality and the Emergence of Complexity: An Analytical Approach. *Journal of Evolutionary Economics*, *24*(2), 317–334. https://doi.org/10.1007/s00191-014-0342-z.

Muñoz, F.-F., & Encinar, M. I. (2014b). Agents' Intentionality, Capabilities, and the Performance of Systems of Innovation. *Innovation: Management, Policy & Practice*, *16*(1), 71–81. https://doi.org/10.5172/impp.2014.16.1.71.

Muñoz, F.-F., & Encinar, M. I. (2019). Some Elements for a Definition of an Evolutionary Efficiency Criterion. *Journal of Evolutionary Economics*, *29* (3), 919–937. https://doi.org/10.1007/s00191-019-00608-z.

Muñoz, F.-F., Encinar, M. I., & Cañibano, C. (2011). On the Role of Intentionality in Evolutionary Economic Change. *Structural Change and Economic Dynamics*, *22*(3), 193–203. https://doi.org/10.1016/j.strueco.2011.04.002.

Nelson, R. R., & Winter, S. G. (1982). *An Evolutionary Theory of Economic Change*. Cambridge, MA: Harvard University Press.

North, D. C. (1990). *Institutions, Institutional Change, and Economic Performance*. Cambridge: Cambridge University Press.

North, D. C. (2005). *Understanding the process of economic change*. Princeton: Princeton University Press.

Paredes Martín, M. d. C. (2007). *Teorías de la intencionalidad*. Madrid: Síntesis.

Pareto, V. (1909[1981]). *Manuel d'Économie Politique*. Paris: Librarie Droz.

Penrose, E. T. (1959). *The Theory of the Growth of the Firm*. Oxford: Basil Blackwell.

Pentland, B. T., Feldman, M. S., Becker, M. C., & Liu, P. (2012). Dynamics of Organizational Routines: A Generative Model. *Journal of Management Studies*, 49(8), 1484–1508. https://doi.org/10.1111/j.1467-6486.2012.01064.x.

Pólya, G. (1945). *How to Solve It: A New Aspect of Mathematical Method*. Princeton: Princeton University Press.

Popper, K. R. (1959 [2002]). *The Logic of Scientific Discovery*. London: Routledge.

Popper, K. R. (1972). *Objective Knowledge: An Evolutionary Approach*. Oxford: Oxford University Press.

Popper, K. R., & Eccles, J. C. (1977). *The Self and Its Brain: An Argument for Interactionism*. Berlin: Springer.

Potts, J. (2000). *The New Evolutionary Microeconomics: Complexity, Competence and Adaptive Behaviour*. Cheltenham: Edward Elgar.

Rizzo, M. J. (2015). The problem of rationality: Austrian Economics between Classical Behaviorism and Behavioral Economics. In P. J. Boettke & C. J. Coyne (Eds.), *The Oxford Handbook of Austrian Economics* (pp. 364–392). New York: Oxford University Press.

Robbins, L. (1932). *An Essay on the Nature and Significance of Economic Science* (2nd ed., 1969). London: Macmillan.

Rosenbaum, E. (2022). Mental Models and Institutional Inertia. *Journal of Institutional Economics*, *18*(3), 361–378. https://doi.org/10.1017/S174413742100059X.

Rosser, J. B. J. (Ed.) (2004). *Complexity in Economics. Methodology, Interacting Agents and Microeconomic Models*. Cheltenham: Edward Elgar.

Rubio de Urquía, R. (2005). La naturaleza y estructura fundamental de la teoría económica y las relaciones entre enunciados teórico-económicos y enunciados antropológicos. In R. Rubio de Urquía, E. M. Ureña, & F.-F. Muñoz (Eds.), *Estudios de Teoría Económica y Antropología* (pp. 23–198). Madrid: Instituto de Investigaciones Económicas y Sociales Francisco de Vitoria-AEDOS-Unión Editorial.

Savage, L. J. (1951). The Theory of Statistical Decision. *Journal of the American Statistical Association*, *46*, 55–67.

Schelling, T. C. (1978). *Micromotives and macrobehaviors*. New York: W. W. Norton.

Schumpeter, J. A. (1943 [1996]). *Capitalism, Socialism and Democracy*. London: Routledge.

Schumpeter, J. A. (1947). The Creative Response in Economic History. *Journal of Economic History*, *7*, 149–159.

Schutz, A. (1943). The Problem of Rationality in the Social World. *Economica*, *10*(38), 130–149. https://doi.org/10.2307/2549460.

Schutz, A. (1951). Choosing among Projects of Action. *Philosophy and Phenomenological Research*, *12*(2), 161–184. https://doi.org/10.2307/2103478.

Searle, J. R. (1983). *Intentionality: An Essay in the Philosophy of Mind*. Cambridge: Cambridge University Press.

Searle, J. R. (1995). *The Construction of Social Reality*. New York: The Free Press.

Searle, J. R. (2001). *Rationality in Action*. Cambridge, MA: The MIT Press.

Searle, J. R. (2005). What is an Institution? *Journal of Institutional Economics*, *1*(1), 1–22. https://doi.org/10.1017/S1744137405000020.

Sen, A. K. (1993). Internal Consistency of Choice. *Econometrica*, *61*(3), 495–521. https://doi.org/10.2307/2951715.

Sen, A. K. (2010). Introduction. In R. P. Hanley (Ed.), *The Theory of Moral Sentiments*. New York: Penguin Classics, vii–xxvi.

Shackle, G. L. S. (1972). *Epistemics and Economics: A Critique of Economic Doctrines*. Cambridge: Cambridge University Press.

Shackle, G. L. S. (1979). *Imagination and the Nature of Choice*. Edinburgh: Edinburgh University Press.

Simon, H. A. (1955). A Behavioral Model of Rational Choice. *The Quarterly Journal of Economics*, *69*(1), 99–118.

Simon, H. A. (1969). *The Sciences of the Artificial* (3rd ed.). Cambridge, MA: The MIT Press.

Simon, H. A. (1983). *Reason in Human Affairs*. Stanford: Stanford University Press.

Smith, A. (1776 [1976]). *An Inquiry into the Nature and Causes of the Wealth of Nations*. Oxford: Oxford University Press.

Smith, A. (1795 [1980]). The Principles Which Lead and Direct Philosophical Enquiries: Illustrated by the History of Astronomy. In W. P. D. Wightman (Ed.), *Essays on Philosophical Subjects*. Oxford: Oxford University Press, 31–105.

Soros, G. (2013). Fallibility, Reflexivity, and the Human Uncertainty Principle. *Journal of Economic Methodology*, *20*(4), 309–329. https://doi.org/10.1080/1350178X.2013.859415.

Stackelberg, H. v. (1946] [1943). *Principios de Teoría Económica [Grundzüge der theoretischen Volkwirtschaftslehre] Spanish edition augmented, and revised by the author*. Madrid: Instituto de Estudios Políticos.

Sugden, R. (1991). Rational Choice: A Survey of Contributions from Economics and Philosophy. *The Economic Journal*, *101*(407), 751–785. https://doi.org/10.2307/2233854.

Sugden, R. (2005). Why Rationality Is Not a Consequence of Hume's Theory of Choice. *European Journal of the History of Economic Thought*, *12*(1), 113–118. https://doi.org/10.1080/0967256042000338069.

Teece, D. J., Pisano, G., & Shuen, A. (1997). Dynamic Capabilities and Strategic Management. *Strategic Management Journal*, *18*(7), 509–533.

Tesfatsion, L. (2021). Agent-Based Computational Economics: Overview and Brief History. *Economics Working Papers: Department of Economics, Iowa State University, 21004*.

Thaler, R. H. (2015). *Misbehaving: The Making of Behavioral Economics*. New York: W.W. Norton.

Tinbergen, J. (1961). Do Communist and Free Economies Show a Converging Pattern? *Soviet Studies*, *12*(4), 333–341.

Tomasello, M., Carpenter, M., Call, J., Behne, T., & Moll, H. (2005). Understanding and Sharing Intentions: The Origins of Cultural Cognition. *Behavioral and Brain Sciences*, *28*, 675–691. https://doi.org/10.1017/S0140525X05000129.

Vanberg, V. J. (2022). Carl Menger, F.A. Hayek and the Evolutionary Strand in Austrian Economics. *The Review of Austrian Economics*, *35*(4), 481–515.

Viale, R. (Ed.) (2027). *The Elgar Handbook of Cognitive Economics*. Cheltenham: Edward Elgar.

Wagner, R. E. (2010). *Mind, Society, and Human Action: Time and Knowledge in a Theory of Social Economy*. London: Routledge.

Wagner, R. E. (2012). A Macro Economy as an Ecology of Plans. *Journal of Economic Behavior & Organization*, *82*(2–3), 433–444. https://doi.org/10.1016/j.jebo.2011.07.019.

Wagner, R. E. (2020). *Macroeconomics as Systems Theory. Transcending the Micro-Macro Dichotomy*. Cham: Palgrave Macmillan.

Weintraub, E. R. (1979). *Microfoundations. The Compatibility of Microeconomics and Macroeconomics*. Cambridge: Cambridge University Press.

Witt, U. (2003). *The Evolving Economy*. Cheltenham: Edward Elgar.

Witt, U. (2008). What is Specific about Evolutionary Economics? *Journal of Evolutionary Economics*, *18*, 547–575.

Ziman, J. (1978). *Reliable Knowledge*. Cambridge: Cambridge University Press.

Ziman, J. (2000). *Real Science: What it is, and what it means*. Cambridge: Cambridge University Press.

Cambridge Elements

Evolutionary Economics

About the Series

Cambridge Elements of Evolutionary Economics provides authoritative and up-to-date reviews of core topics and recent developments in the field. It includes state-of-the-art contributions on all areas in the field. The series is broadly concerned with questions of dynamics and change, with a particular focus on processes of entrepreneurship and innovation, industrial and institutional dynamics, and on patterns of economic growth and development.

Cambridge Elements

Evolutionary Economics

Elements in the Series

A full series listing is available at: www.cambridge.org/EEVE

Printed in the United Kingdom by TJ Clays Ltd.